HEALING FROM RACIAL DISCRIMINATION!

¿AHORA QUÉ? NOW, WHAT?

7 Strategies for Navigating and Healing from Discrimination in the Workplace

ARACELI ESPARZA

FORWARD BY
CLAUDIA ROMO EDLEMAN

ARACELI ♥ ESPARZA

TABLE OF CONTENTS

DEDICATION

I dedicate this book to my mother (Sylvia Lopez), Mi Abuelita (Zeferina M. Lopez), and her mother, Trinidad. I want to pay honor to Mi Tío Pancho del Rancho, who passed away during the time I wrote this book. I also dedicate this book to my son, daughter, y mi esposo amoroso, Bruno, my siblings, friends, mentors, and supporters. I'm grateful to God, and my ancestors, who have helped me in this vida loca.

My family's support is pivotal for me because of them; I've had the freedom to write and the inspiration to continue despite the setbacks that workplace harassment and discrimination have caused us.

I dedicate this book to every Chicana, Mexicana, Latina, immigrant, and Brown woman living in the Midwest who has felt isolated from her community and culture.

I tell you with all my heart:

No Estas Sola, No Estas Sola, No Estas Sola,

Ni Estas Loca, Es Racismo.

You are not alone, You are not alone, You are not alone,

You're not crazy; it's called racism.

ACKNOWLEDGMENTS

I couldn't have done this work without the great unity and support of my family, and so many men and women in Wisconsin. I dedicate this book to my community for your unwavering support. And I couldn't do this work without the beautiful land on which we live. Our land is in great danger because of global warming—these beautiful hills, lakes, and woodlands might be gone, if we don't protect them. We must act now to protect our planet, our home. I couldn't have done it without you, planet Earth.

I also want to thank the City of Madison Equal Opportunities Commission for their silent dedication to the witnessing of discrimination cases that are handled by the EEOC's Chicago District Office, which has jurisdiction over Illinois, Wisconsin, Minnesota, Iowa, North Dakota, and South Dakota, with area offices in Milwaukee and Minneapolis. Weekly, as a commission, we are sent notifications of cases settled by the EEOC office. It's astounding to see how much money is lost each year to discrimination cases in our area, but it's also a shock at the variety of ways that people are so mean to each other. Our tiny Commission may seem unimportant, but last year we were Zoom bombed twice by white supremacists who thought it was funny to attack one of our great Black women leaders.

I can't talk about discrimination in the workplace without acknowledging the real violence that is being brought on people of color every day. This book is for all the people who have died because of racial discrimination, bias, genocide, hate, and racism in our country and the world.

The words in this book are my opinion and not representative of anyone mentioned in this book.

DISCLAIMER

B efore we begin, I'm not a lawyer or a mental health professional, and I'm not a licensed social worker. No information contained in this book should be considered as legal advice. The information and other content provided in this book, or any linked materials, are not intended and should not be construed as medical or mental health advice. If you are experiencing trauma or are in crisis, call or text 988 to connect with a trained crisis counselor 24/7. Or access this site: https://projectlets.org/resources.

FOREWORD

Araceli Esparza first came to my attention as a contributor to our annual publication of *Hispanic Stars Rising*, which the We Are All Human Foundation created to combat stereotypes of Latinos and raise awareness of our contributions and achievements. Araceli shared her journey, with its frustrations and accomplishments, and it was clear that she was well on her way to an interesting next chapter. That is where we find Araceli today, making a new and important contribution with the publication of her book *Healing from Racial Discrimination! ¿Ahora Que? Now, What?*

Araceli's book is filling a real need, responding to an all too commonplace problem, and I applaud her courage. Latinas occupy a complicated place in American society. We are highly educated—a young demographic with a long future ahead of us in the workplace. And we are fueling the economy with Latinas making 80% of household purchasing decisions. Latino purchasing power is currently at $3.4 trillion. That is an extraordinary amount.

Latina power is fueling the economy, but our power has yet to be felt or fully respected in the workplace, which partially explains why the rate of Latina entrepreneurship outpaces all other groups. In contrast, in the corporate world, Latinas make up only 2% of senior executive roles. Data shows that an overwhelming majority of Latinas do not feel comfortable being themselves at work. The lack of representation makes it difficult to find role models or mentors. Stereotypes silence Latinas, human resources, or managers and cut off opportunities for leadership and mentorship. Misperceptions encourage us to be mute and passive. All this underlying discomfort diminishes engagement and deprives intelligent, insightful, and innovative Latinas of the established career paths and support that other men and women typically find. It is counterintuitive for companies as well, which are also depriving their businesses of the benefits of diverse thinking, multicultural perspectives, and, quite frankly, the commitment and loyalty that often supercharge corporate objectives.

In the past five years, however, we have begun to see a change, and Araceli's efforts are emblematic of this. More and more Latinos are embracing our Latinidad—embracing our origins, our heritage, our resilience, and our values. We are seeing a real surge in the Spanish language, coming mainly from the younger generations born in the States. With all this comes a palpable sense of pride in the community and a newfound confidence.

I have been encouraging young women to flip the script—to take the tired stereotypes and turn them on their end. We are not loud; we are enthusiastic and passionate about what we do. Yes, we are family-minded, but that makes us great team players who are empathetic and attuned to others. And yes, we are enormously diverse, which gives us real insights into understanding not only a multicultural society that more and more defines America but also a global marketplace.

I am confident that we will drive positive change. But with this must also come the ability and will to fight injustice along the way. Araceli's book is informative and intelligent. What's more, it lights a needed spark of activism, creating agency in our own lives. If you find yourself being discriminated against, you will find strength and support in Araceli's own experience, and most importantly, you will find her book to be a clear and concise handbook that empowers you. It isn't easy to speak up, but this book will help you find your voice and fight the good fight. Along the way, you just might discover your inner strengths and some great qualities that make you uniquely you. Stay positive. Find your allies. Build your community. And most of all, help the next person. Start this journey by learning from Araceli.

Claudia Romo Edelman is a global mobilization expert, catalyst for social change, and marketer for social causes. She is a recognized speaker, media contributor, and inspiring activist. The Founder & CEO of the We Are All Human Foundation, Claudia is also the co-host of the podcast A la Latina: the playbook to succeed being your authentic self.

Claudia Romo Edleman, Founder and CEO of the Hispanic Star Host of A LA LATINA

IG: @claudiaromoedelman
LI: Claudia Romo Edelman

INTRODUCTION

"I knew it when white people would treat me better than mi Abuelita.

I knew it when social services threatened to take us away from my mom when they told her, "This isn't Mexico. You can't treat your kids this way."

G rowing up in Wisconsin as a first-generation Chicana (a Latina from Mexican origin) gives me the expertise to talk about racism; I have witnessed it firsthand since I was a child. What I describe above is colorism, racism, economic discrimination, and immigration intimidation. It's layered because I love Mi Mamá, and when social services came to our house that day, in low-income housing, threatening us the way they did, I knew they were not there to help.

Writing a book about racial discrimination in the nonprofit industry is needed; often, Latinas are lured into these entry-level jobs, thinking they can change poverty with a barely getting-by salary. However, the reality is that these jobs often come with a culture of tokenization, abuse, and pitting against each other, which can be particularly challenging for Latinas, and women of color, and any one from a marginalized background. This book aims to shed light on the abuse of racial discrimination and provide strategies for healing and empowerment.

Big Breath.

Being a survivor is in my DNA. I'm a third-generation single parent (my grandma, mom, and me). Before getting fired, I had been a single parent for eight years and worked numerous jobs. But never was I treated in such a way as this, experiencing humiliation, being blindsided, shamed, and disempowered to this extent. Only when it was over did I notice how familiar the abuse was. Yet, I stand here today, a testament to the resilience that lies within each of us.

Racial harassment and racial discrimination is abuse. As a survivor of domestic abuse, incest, poverty, homelessness, mental health, and things that were set to kill or disempower me, I persevered and became a survivor with determination. This endurance has given me skills that I hope to share with you and guide you to healing from the consequences of this racist society.

In this healing journey, I will be that amiga you can trust, with strategies and wisdom as old as onions and garlic sizzling on mi abuelita's pan. Believing that I could be a reflection of love was how I pulled out the thorns from my angry heart. I began to heal by writing, reading, and creating new stories and some good music. These activities helped me process my experiences and find my voice, and I believe they can do the same for you. I hope these tips will serve you well. It's vital that you heal from this job loss because it will happen again. If you are a Latina who desires to do creative or corporate work or become an entrepreneur, you will encounter racism or discrimination, bullying, or some other form of sabotage. And we need you. The future of Latinas needs you to bounce back stronger!

I'm in the healing process for life, por vida. As a young adult, I survived by overthinking and imagining every possible outcome. Then, after having my miracle baby after six miscarriages, I took this contemplative writing class, and that started my healing through writing. I went back to school, got my MFA, and held my first writing class in 2013 in Englewood Public Library in New Jersey. It was such a great experience. Teaching others about your zone of expertise is a great way to heal and feel validated. From poetry to self-discovery workshops, holding healing spaces for folks, creating altars, and building rituals in my daily life, it has helped ground and heal me.

In this book, I'll guide you through the seven strategies for overcoming discrimination in the workplace. Why am I the right person to help you in your healing journey from racial discrimination? I've been through it in various work settings, but the one that hurt me the most was in nonprofit work because the work of social justice is part of my passion and dedication to building resilient communities and Latina empowerment. I want to share my story so that you can discover how to ease the isolation, shame, and disempowerment that comes from being fired due to discrimination.

As a community social service provider, I witnessed many people's stories about workplace discrimination. I am a long-time community organizer and curandera, a traditional healer in the Mexican and Latin American cultures, like mi abuelita before me, who used herbs, teas, y sobadas (healing massages). I use writing and deep empathy to help women see their own stories. I am keen on patterns, and I aim to break these patterns in our family.

The legal process is part of the healing, but your mental health and well-being have no price. It goes beyond a check. That is why I will tell you that if you never file a claim, that's okay. I didn't file the first time it happened to me—when I was fired for having blue hair at JcPenny's at the age of 16, or when I was bullied for being poor and living in public housing when I was 27, or when I was 35 and dismissed for poor performance when in fact I connected over 25 people to employment in less than a month. In all of those moments I didn't file, until finally, at 43 and was harassed to the point that my body created a cyst on my breast. Then I filed.

This book is more than just a collection of strategies. It's a guide, a companion on your journey to healing. I am here to validate the pain that many women of color feel during and after being fired due to workplace discrimination. Your journey is important, and I am here to support you every step of the way.

My book is meant to give you strategies to heal and overcome the emotionally abusive scars that racial discrimination leaves us. These strategies are not just theoretical, but they are born out of my own experiences and the experiences of those I have worked with. It's a roadmap to empowerment and healing, a resource you can turn to whenever you need it.

Now, I would like to share with you what I have been sharing with friends and other nonprofit colleagues over these past years.

Hello! My name is Araceli Esparza.

In 2019, I found myself in an elevator crying; I was shaking with adrenaline and pure violence.

The Chola teenage delinquent, a persona I had worked so hard to suppress, came out, and she wanted revenge.

She wanted blood.

At that moment, I felt my grandmother's hand on my shoulder.

I could hear her telling me, "Ari,… ponlo en las manos de Dios" (Ari, put this in God's hands).

The elevator door opened, and the woman I had chased out of this party was not there.

Instead of looking for her, I walked straight to my car started laughing, crying, and calling my friend.

I drove to her house, and she talked me down.

At that moment I had a choice.

Until this point in my life, I worked as a nonprofit professional for nearly twenty years. But even as a teenager, I was an activist. I was a student protestor, and I was an advocate for abortion rights. I had walked out of my high school and led one of the largest high school student protests of the '90s in my city against police brutality in support of Rodney King. While I was in college, I participated in the Million Man March for

Latinos, a significant event in our fight for equality, in Washington, DC. (Ramos). In my twenties, I helped dozens of Latino families in the Dane County area connect to housing services, medical assistance, and legal advocacy. I even helped people file against discrimination in the workforce.

So, how did I become the target of workplace discrimination and harassment?

How did this single mom who went back to college, finished her bachelor's degree, got married, became homeless for two years, and went back to school to earn a master's degree—how could I fall victim to workplace discrimination, especially in a place that professed social justice?

Not only did I feel ignorant, but I felt utterly discredited. The frustration that I couldn't advocate for myself made me freeze. I don't know if I felt shame so much as humiliation. I felt humiliated that this person had this much power over me. I felt embarrassed that they knew so much about me and used it against me.

Did I feel shame? It's not easy to explain. Perhaps I feel some guilt because of my economic class: working poor or not knowing that it was happening when it was happening. I do know that many people feel ashamed for being undocumented, for working in a low-paying job, for having priors (prior convictions), for being on papers (probation or parole), for being an addict, and none of these things justify being racially discriminated or discriminated by any means.

I devoted many hours to this social justice work because it was my passion. I thought I was making a difference in our community. I felt I could somehow eradicate poverty by working at a nonprofit organization. I'm writing this book because half of Latinos in the US experienced some form of discrimination during the first 12 months of the pandemic.

I wish I could tell you that the numbers before the pandemic were any better, but they weren't. It's not necessary as a Chicana for me to explicitly tell you that I am a citizen of the United States, but for context, I'm sharing. First, let's define what is a Chicana. A Chicana is a woman of Mexican-American descent who was born in the United States. A Chicana also honors our indigenous background, and some are social justice-minded. The fact that I'm a US citizen makes it easier for me to talk about workplace discrimination.

As a bilingual social service provider, I assisted many immigrants by connecting them to lawyers and worker rights advocate centers. I feel very strongly about immigrant rights. Immigrants have the human right to live in our country. Being an immigrant does not give businesses the right to discriminate against or abuse them. The bottom line is that they are people. All people have a right to work in a place free of harassment and bullying. If I were undocumented, my story would have been a hundred times worse.

Let me be clear. The woman who attacked me and harassed me used everything about me, including my Latina-Chicana immigrant background. She used the fact that I was bilingual, and she weaponized all of these things. If I had been undocumented, it would have been worse. She probably would have hit me. There were times when she aggressively came into my office and slammed the door; she would slam her hands on my desk, and she would yell and scream at me to leave her office. I know there are undocumented Mexican, Central American, Caribbean, African, or South American workers right now who are probably being beaten, not to mention the new wave of immigrant workers that are coming to the Midwest from the Middle East, Africa, South American, or Asia, and are probably being abused.

We tolerate all of this for the almighty dollar.

When Latinas y Latinos face discrimination, we don't report the violations. It has a lot to do with our community and our culture, and that's exactly why I'm writing this book: to break this isolation and uncover the notion that we are good workers—yes, we are—and we are good at keeping quiet.

That part ends now.

I am willing to be the chismosa, the wakcalera, and La Malinche in this story. It's safe for me to tell my story on my terms. I don't have to hide anymore. I don't fear retaliation from the nonprofit industry or from my own community. I'm doing the work. I'm using what I've learned in my healing journey to empower women on a national level.

Today, I am helping other Mujeres use their stories for personal gain. As Black and Latina professionals get more comfortable telling their stories, more programs and funding will be offered to build resiliency in our communities. So, we can have less crimes of poverty, less hate, and more culturally rooted mental health services. The work of healing needs to be on a community-wide level. And this is where I need your help! YES, Amiga YOU! You are part of this movement! We need you to build yourself up again and tap into your genius, but first, let's do a couple of mini-limpias, a little clearing of the soul and rooting inward.

I want to help women liberate their stories so they can end the self-pain we do to ourselves. We've got to stop worrying about what others think about us and what they are doing to block our advancement. In no way have I attained some higher level. Heck no! I'm still being blocked; I still suffer from bouts of messy crying and pits of low self-esteem. Storytelling is one way I heal; there are many ways to heal, as we will learn in this book.

Yes. Mujer, **you**, I'm here to help you free your voice. **Tu voz** es importante. Tu voz tiene valor. No es facil. Yo se que tienes miedo. Yo se que te sientes sola. Your voice is important and valuable. It won't be easy, and you may feel fearful and alone, but you will get through it.

In this book, there will be times when I switch back and forth from English to Spanish. When I switch to Spanish, that's the heart. That's the real corazón, that mother heart, that Abuelita heart, that chocolate, that atole.

I miss my grandmother. You have to know she saved my life, and if it weren't for her, I probably would have never gone to college, and I wouldn't have learned about racial discrimination. She literally prepared me for all of this.

Growing up, I would hear about how my grandmother was racially discriminated against at the University, where she was a janitor for so many years. The students would draw pictures of her on the walls; they would act as if she didn't know English. When, in fact, she did know English. She would laugh about it because she was embarrassed to speak it, but it didn't mean she didn't understand what they were trying to do to her. Every morning at 5 AM, she took a bus to work. She was also part of the Union, and she told me that if she paid these people, perhaps it meant that they couldn't fire her completely.

I wrote this book for you Chicana, for you Latina, for you recent immigrants, for those of you who don't have a college education, and for those who have been discriminated against. I wrote it for all of you who have ever felt like you finally got hired for your dream job, only to be completely treated like crap and dismissed and humiliated in front of your peers. This book is for those of you whom everyone expects great things from but who are mistreated and blamed when you complain or try to change.

I wrote this book for the many women who have left a job or were fired by had no proof of discrimination. If you ever felt disempowered in how you let go, I wrote this book for you. You don't need a college education, nor do you need a high school education to know when you are being demeaned because of the color of your skin, because of your gender, your sexual orientation, your immigrant background, or for telling your story. I see you.

You are worthy of any job you want and capable of doing the job you were hired for. Of all the things they said to me about my race, the slick and demeaning way they referenced my immigrant background and my language, the one thing that stuck with me, even to this day, is how they wrote in an email to the board and me that I was underqualified for my job.

Mi sueño is that through this book, you will find your voice and be empowered to take action. I am writing to break the isolation of workplace discrimination in the nonprofit sector as a Latina or person of color! I also included tips and action strategies to help you heal.

For organizations or study groups, I have included discussion questions at the end of the chapters for you to dive into as a group. Remember to use I statements, make agreements or ground rules, and no self-disparaging comments! Take time in your group discussions.

This is heavy work.

CHAPTER 1

MONKEY MIND AND SKELETON HAND: CHALLENGE YOUR INNER CRITIC

The first step in healing from racial discrimination in the workplace is to know you aren't alone. The inner critic, or the skeleton hand, will isolate you into thinking you are not good enough, or the monkey mind will have you believe you have bad luck.

In my workshops, I use these two symbols—the 'skeleton hand' representing the inner critic that tells us false stories about who we are and the 'monkey mind' that jumps from one thing to another—to embody the two things we face in our healing journey. These metaphors help us identify and challenge limiting beliefs and break the isolation that may be hard to recognize on our own.

"Every terrorist regime in the world uses isolation to break people's spirits.

But love is really more of an interactive process.

It's about what we do, not just what we feel."

-bell hooks

I hope this book is an interactive process for you, where you can open any part and take the steps you need. Remember two things: we all have a monkey mind that jumps from one thing to another and the skeleton hand that is your inner critic. I have found it helpful to imagine these two representations when I feel alone. Yes, you might feel alone now, but how much of that is true?

You might need help finding a new job, but does that mean you are not talented?

The Journey

As you navigate this journey, your emotional and mental well-being will be your north star. Doing it alone is not advisable. You may be thinking, but who can I trust? I know I tried to do it by myself, leading to another failed job and a waste of time. That is why it is so essential for you to know that according to a 2017 Pew Research Center survey, 42% of working women in the United States have experienced gender discrimination in the workplace and feel they have been treated differently based on their gender. You are not alone. Women and many others have been made to believe that discrimination is something that we can prevent or that we caused it due to our "poor" work performance. That is not the whole story. Gaslighting us into silence or staying complacent in an abusive workplace does not work anymore.

You can heal from this experience and regain your footing in whatever job you want next. Part of knowing that you are valuable involves talking to your ancestors and your family. They've gone through racist experiences. Maybe they're going through racial discrimination right now, or they did recently, and you could talk to them about it. The skeleton hand wants you to think you have bad luck or una mancha, but you don't! This is not your fault, and part of knowing that you're not alone is also knowing that it's not your fault. The monkey mind will have you double-thinking your actions. But remember, you have the power to heal and reclaim your worth.

You did nothing wrong to perpetuate, instigate, or bring this upon yourself. It's not about whether or not you weren't qualified to do the work. They chose their words and actions to either disempower or humiliate you or sabotage you based on your race, your gender, or your background. They used your background or disability against you, and they perpetuated the stereotypes that are out there.

Black people and Latinos are often thought of as lazy people in our community. They're thought of as natural aggressors for the perpetrator. It's the justification of discrimination. Firing us is seen as a natural solution because we have to be put in our place. We're just crazy people. God knows what will happen to us or what we will do.

The Stereotypes

Latinas are often not thought of as intelligent people, that skeletonhand again. We are thought of as sexy and spicy or prompted as a role model for speaking perfect English (Don't call me exotic: terms to stop using that sexualize Latinas). Even the former president of the United States sees us as unworthy and criminals—yes, even the president. Don't dwell on these stereotypes either, but it's important to know they do exist. The people who do care about you will see you as a whole person.

Employers know what the public perception of Latinos is. All Latinas are immigrants, and we are out to steal your job, and we are only good at caretaking, etc.. Common misconceptions: culturally, Latinas are all the same; we only know how to work at home, we are great cooks, and we are loud and obnoxious. Human Resource people know this. They know the stereotypes about us. So when we come out to talk about discrimination or harassment on the job or to make a complaint, they are not there to advocate for our rights.

Building Community

Your friends, family, allies, and colleagues in other organizations will be the ones who can help you through this. Your friends might even be white women. Fair warning: your friends might be friends with the person who harmed you. Especially in the nonprofit industry, everyone knows each other. That happened to me. Nobody wanted to talk to me about it, but I found a few people who did, and I am forever grateful for those folks. Remember, you are not alone in this journey. Building a community of support is crucial in overcoming racial discrimination in the workplace.

They're the ones who held me when I was crying. They are the ones who told me to file for discrimination, and they basically told me all the same things I had told so many people before. Their support and my resilience in the face of discrimination are a testament to our strength and capability.

There's a Puerto Rican author, Aurora Levin Morales, whose work I enjoy. She has an approach to writing stories where she guides us on how to write about our histories when there isn't any evidence. She says that the lack of evidence for women's shaped holes in our history doesn't mean it didn't happen. Just because you don't have substantial evidence of racial discrimination doesn't mean it didn't happen (Levin Morales, 1998).

Remember, just because there might not be solid evidence that you were discriminated against, it doesn't mean it didn't happen. As women, we've often faced mistreatment without having substantial evidence, but we know our truth. It's disappointing to think that people wouldn't support you or that you feel alone after doing so much work in our community. But remember, you are not alone, and you have the power to heal and reclaim your worth.

As an organizer, advocate, social worker, community connector, manager, or executive director of a nonprofit organization, you have helped many people, but have you really helped yourself? Remember that skeleton hand? It tends to want to rob our joy. The monkey mind will instead fault our actions and move on because we have to make money rather than spend time on healing. Healing is essential to getting the job you want and creating the workplace in which you are validated. Mujer, it's time to sit down with yourself and welcome in healthy love— the love that calls in all of your gifts, talents, insights, and dreams. You've been a good friend, hija, mama, tia, community activist, social worker, teacher, nurse, and any other helping professional, and now it's time to be a good friend to yourself.

What is racial discrimination?

▶ Race discrimination involves treating someone (an applicant or employee) unfavorably because they are of a certain race or because of personal characteristics associated with race (such as hair texture, skin color, or certain facial features). Color discrimination involves treating someone unfavorably because of skin color complexion.

▶ *Race/color discrimination can also involve treating someone unfavorably because the person is married to (or associated with) a person of a certain race or color.*

▶ *Discrimination can occur when the victim and the person who inflicted the discrimination are of the same race or color (U.S. Equal Employment Opportunity Commission, n.d.).*

The best example is giving Black or Brown folks longer hours on the job than everyone else, even when the supervisor is a woman of color. It is still discrimination. Typically, there are red flags before the discrimination actually happens. But in some cases, it happens immediately from day one. Listen to your instincts, question, or ask your friends what they think about questionable behavior.

What is racial harassment?

- It is unlawful to harass a person because of that person's race or color.

- Harassment can include, for example, racial slurs, offensive or derogatory remarks about a person's race or color, or the display of racially offensive symbols.

Although the law doesn't prohibit simple teasing, offhand comments, or isolated incidents that are not very serious, harassment is illegal when it is so frequent or severe that it creates a hostile or offensive work environment or when it results in an adverse employment decision (such as the victim being fired or demoted). As if we Latinas don't have enough to handle, harassment is particularly good at confirming your inner critic about your worth.

The Drama

The harasser can be the victim's supervisor, a supervisor in another area, a co-worker, or someone who is not an employee of the employer, such as a client or customer (U.S. Equal Employment Opportunity Commission).

When the person who racially harassed me in 2019 said to me that it felt like we were from two different planets, it was simple teasing, right? It wasn't. Consider that she knew I was first-generation and bilingual. They used that information to intimidate me. My need for approval and acceptance mentally made me jump away from letting it ruin my life at the time. However, my case was missing the adverse employment decision or action. That didn't happen until later.

Something that helped me recently is researching the effects of workplace trauma. I think you'll agree that just reading what pops up is important. I know I blamed myself, but it wasn't my fault. The skeleton hand will like to tell you that you did this and that you can't move or improve who you are.

These are complicated issues. If you are reading this and it's triggering you, that's natural. Remember that Bell Hooks quote? Healing like love is an interactive action. The process takes reflection, and noticing. Notice how this has changed you.

Reflections

Have you been hiding the racial discrimination that you went through because you don't want everybody else to think you're a failure? Have you kept it a secret because you don't think people will believe you?

I believe you. More people will believe you if you tell them. Don't let the Monkey mind brush this off.

Your workplace discrimination affects groups of people around you, including, but not limited to, your family, your friends, neighborhoods, and people at your local market. Even if you are a single person, there are people in your life who are going through this with you, even your pets are experiencing your sadness, frustration, and anger.

My plants were suffering during this time because I wasn't watering them. My whole body was suffering because I wasn't taking care of it. I grew a cyst on my left breast, and it's still there. I had to get it checked out for breast cancer prematurely. My racial discrimination or harassment happened when I was 42 years old, and I had this cyst grow on the side of my breast that my body created due to the stress. It reminds me daily that I need to take care of myself.

Lessons

As a speaker and consultant to nonprofit organizations, I teach about intersectionality and how to avoid burnout by cultivating a personal mission for front-line workers or social service providers. When I begin a workshop or talk, I like to start with a mindfulness activity that will harness the best version of the people in the audience. I hope these healing activities and action strategies will serve you and strengthen your walk on this journey.

Healing from Racial discrimination is a lifelong journey. When you are in these circumstances, it's hard to determine who can help you and who is a friend. We will talk more about how to build a support system in later chapters. For now, be easy on yourself. Don't blame or shame yourself. Part of the healing process is defining or learning the landscape. The following section will cover steps to center yourself and some action steps.

Take some clearing breaths with a brave heart as you take the next steps.

Healing Activity:

▶ When you begin a mindful activity, remember to take some clearing breaths that will help regulate your nervous system. I have found using the Box breathing technique helpful. Box breathing, also known as four-square breathing, is a simple breathing technique that can help relieve stress and improve concentration (University of Arizona, n.d.). It involves:

▶ Breathing in slowly for a count of four

▶ Holding your breath for four seconds

▶ Exhaling slowly for a count of four

▶ Holding your breath for four seconds at the bottom of your exhale

Action Strategies

1. Start writing down what happened in a stream-of-consciousness or random order and then go back and arrange it chronologically. It doesn't have to be perfect. Write down at least two or three things that they did. Now, here's the important part: Write down if there were any witnesses. Write down exactly what they said to you or did. Or do an audio voice memo on your phone.

2. Search online for information on how to file a discrimination report in your city. You don't have to file right now. Research the time limits for filing. You have a certain amount of time to file after the incident. I want you to look at how you can file. Give yourself permission to Google about racial discrimination.

3. Locate your civil rights office and ask them about the process for making a complaint.

4. Again, this is hard work, reach out to a friend to talk with. Don't get yourself in a bundle just yet.

    a. It's not about whether or not you have a case. At this point, it's just the simple act of looking for legal help. We will discuss, in detail in later chapters, why filing is such an important action.

Discussion Questions for Groups

We all have these tapes in our heads of stereotypes of not believing women of color. In particular, Black and Latina women. Ask yourself, why is that? And finally, for all of the Latinas reading this, ask yourself, *quien te enseño*. Who taught you to keep a secret? And why?

1. How are you actively helping women of color in your community?

2. How can white women and men be an ally to women of color without causing harm?

3. Think of all the times that you have heard a hard-to-believe workplace story from a Black or Latina woman, and ask yourself: why is it so easy for me **not** to believe them? Why was it so easy for me to cast doubt on their statement?

Ahora Tú: Reflect & Release

CHAPTER 2

LEAN ON YOUR CARE NETWORK

This chapter will review what a good peer support or ally is and what that looks and feels like. Being a micro-influencer has helped me and hurt me in finding a care network. There were times when I reached out to "friends" who claimed to be diversity, inclusion, and equity consultants. They shut me out because I triggered them.

Support Systems

Thankfully, I reached out to a local Black female pastor friend, and she counseled me. I could lean on her and ask her for help, and she helped me by listening and validating my experiences. Another friend who studied to be a lawyer and worked for many years in Detroit, Michigan's community social justice area, also counseled me, invited me to her home, and checked up on me. My husband held me, hugged me, and was there for me. He would always tell me, "Que se vaya a la chingada, manda a la chingada!"

Being able to laugh and say those words is funny for Mexican or bilingual people. It helped me to laugh. Laughter is going to help you. In fact, one of my comedian friends was there for me, too. She's a transwoman who is an amazing advocate, and she looked me straight in the eyes. I'll never forget what she said, "You are so worthy; you didn't deserve any of that!" It shouldn't surprise you that other women of color and Latinas might not be there for you.

The very people who witnessed what this person did to you might not support you.

Notice that all the people who supported me were not from the "traditional" community that one may think of but are considered outliers. They were outliers like me. I would rather share with someone who is happy and empathetic, regardless of their education, than someone who is judgemental and cold with a Ph.D. This realization opened my eyes to the fact that your allies are going to be people you wouldn't have thought of. They're going to be people who might have stayed quiet for many years, and once you open up to them, you'll find out a whole other part of their lives that you didn't know.

I often find the people who have helped me the most are people who are simply receiving, and they are holding the space but not necessarily sharing their trauma with you. They respect your trauma, and they appreciate the fact that they are here to witness your pain, not to add to it. Maybe right now, you can't even name someone who can be your ally, support system, or friend because all of your friends, as you know, have never gone through this. Maybe it's hard for you to trust anyone in your city because you're pretty sure they won't believe you and may cause you more harm.

Even when it feels like you're alone in your struggle, remember that you have the power to seek help. On a national level, you can reach out through social media or join a chat forum. Many people are using Reddit and Discord as alternatives to Facebook and LinkedIn. Using social media, you will find allies outside of your typical community. For me, that proactive step helped me pivot and gain support on a national level from my influencer amigas! On the flip side, getting off social is also helpful for healing. Giving yourself silence and solace for your heart and spirit is necessary for healing.

Online Community

 Many times, I have anonymously listened to a webinar that I found on Eventbrite, which is an additional tool to use. Go to Eventbrite and

look for conversations about workplace discrimination. Even listening to others talk about workplace discrimination and harassment is a way to find an ally.

On LinkedIn, I've talked about the importance of workplace emotional safety, and every time I mention it, Mujeres ask me how they can "pivot" from their current role to being a jefa. We talk about the pain of being invisible. Being Latina means you will be given less—less money, less time off, and less downtime. I thought nonprofits were giving Latinas a better start than corporations, but given my experience, I have reevaluated this position.

What I've learned is Latinas need a collaborative work environment to thrive. Given our international roots, some of us come from oppressive countries that had dictatorships. We thrive in work environments where our mission and the organization's mission align. This means that if our cultural values, such as family, future generations, and inclusion, are represented in the organization's company culture, then we will thrive.

The bottom line is our allies aren't always obvious. It is a little bit of work, and yes, it's so hard to look for people to help you when you feel like crap, but you're reading this right now, and that's a good step! You and I are forming your community right now. Remember, support groups and mental health centers are good places to check out support as well. The key is to keep an open mind and be willing to look for allies in unexpected places. You'll be surprised at the people who step up to support you.

How did this global historical movement of racial uprising and the pandemic (George Floyd and Black Lives) help me find my allies?

It did in so many different ways. It ignited my interest in discussing anti-blackness in the Latino community (check out YT Channel @ MidwestMujeres). I hosted and produced several Zoom talks. I held conversations amongst Latino artists to talk about their work in the community and how it ties to social justice. Many people were motivated to equip others with tools so they could be part of the solution. Diversity, equity, and inclusion were on fire! Hundreds of businesses were creating positions to help bring social change for Black and Brown people in professional spaces.

Shortly after, I stumbled upon a post from a Latina in Milwaukee, about a free certification course on diversity, and inclusion. Seeking ways to validate my intelligence and credibility, I stumbled upon a post from a Latina in Milwaukee offering a free certification course on diversity and inclusion. This was the start of my journey towards self-education and empowerment. I threw myself into the online course in 2021, along with thousands of students, and received a free certification from the University of South Florida Muma College of Business. This experience taught me the power of self-education and how it can empower us to take control of our own narratives.

Pivoting

I decided to become a Diversity and Inclusion consultant. Who better to talk about workplace discrimination than someone who survived it? *The inner critic skeleton hand said to me, "Oh, you're not prepared. You don't have any systems. Who do you think you are to be a consultant? You don't have an MBA; You have an MFA in creative writing for children, and you have dyslexia. Stay in your lane, kid."* These were all the voices that I heard in my head.

Finding your allies is about finding out what kind of people you relate to or are in your community. Perhaps you're a survivor of domestic violence, sexual assault, or incest, or you are a survivor of poverty or homelessness. Maybe the workplace discrimination that you faced is triggering all these other traumas. I think it's time to think about your next move in life. Talking about your next move or journaling about what you want to do next is a great way to name the type of help you need.

When I think back to my Black woman pastor friend, my trans comedian friend, my lawyer friend, and my husband, who made me laugh, I think back at what made them good allies. They didn't judge me. They didn't dump the things that happened to them on me. They made eye contact with me. They didn't push me away but listened to me. Whenever I see them, they smile; they are my cheerleaders, and they make me laugh. Laughter is a unique and beautiful healing medicine.

Asking for Help

Often, people tell us to get help. It can be challenging if we don't know where to seek help. I remember this Latina immigrant woman who came to me looking for work. I told her about a place I heard was hiring. It was a factory where they tested rodents (yeah, I know it was terrible!). She had heard of this place, too, but strangely enough, neither of us knew the name of this place.

She said, "Araceli, you are literally the fourth or fifth person who told me I could get a job at Las Ratas, this laboratory. But what am I supposed to do? Go out in the city and yell, 'Where is Las Ratas?--Where can I work?'

We both started laughing. Society is the same way. They tell us to look for help, but if we don't know where to look, it can be frustrating, and we give up.

Finding a good support network, alliance, or people who will believe in and support you can be frustrating. Unfortunately, it's hard work when you are dealing with a cup half empty. I'm not saying you need to shout it out, but maybe this is the first time you actually thought about what type of help you want to receive. That is a huge step! Just thinking of the type of help you want is a big step.

Healing Activity

▶ Think about how you want to be treated when receiving help. Write 5-10 weather words on a blank page. Then, use some of those words for the following writing prompt.

▶ For example, do you want *help* to be gentle like a breeze, or do you want to be like a volcano erupting and destroying everything so that new things can grow? Using your weather words, describe the help you want.

Action Strategies

1. *Get social, but slowly. We talked about going to different social media forums. Remember, you can remain anonymous.*

2. *Be aware of your ability to share and when to share. As people say, "Boundaries are Beautiful." When you prepare to share, consider asking them: "Hey, I want to share with you something deep, and I want to warn you about it. Is it okay to share?"*

3. *Come up with a preface before you tell your story that allows them to say no. We can't imagine all of the other traumas they might have, and if they are not healed from those things, it could cause more harm. Trauma sharing isn't productive for you right now.*

4. *Become an ally for a cause that you believe in. For me, it's social justice, so I started becoming vocal about it—about Latina's wage gap, racial discrimination, and the anti-blackness in the Latino community. It was something that I could talk about. By talking about my passion, I was able to find other like-minded people. Eventually, we spoke of workplace discrimination and other similar topics. Talking to more people was healing and continues to help me figure out my next step.*

Discussion Questions for Groups

1. *Why is trauma bonding unproductive for the healing journey?*

2. *Who are natural allies in your community?*

3. *Name three things that you think make for a good ally.*

Ahora Tú: Reflect & Release

CHAPTER 3

KNOW YOUR RIGHTS

Know your rights
You have a right to be sad
You have a right to be angry
You have the right to be silent.
You have the right to scream
You have the right to be frustrated
You have the right to do nothing
You have the right to pursue another job, even though it may not be the best idea right now.
You have the right to pause
You have the right to yell in your car while you're driving down the street.
You have the right to smile
You have the right to laugh
You have the right to screw up,
You have the right to have the Blues,
You have the right to cry,
You have the right to shake
You have the right to go on a vacation,
You have a right to heal.

Processing all of these emotions is not going to happen at once. Do not rush the process. This journey is not linear. Healing takes time, and just when you think you're done, another wound or challenge will arise. Although the body can heal itself from stress, it will still physically respond to stress, and it can even cause sickness. Shaking, crying, trembling, and getting a knot in your stomach are all regular reactions. The body is protecting itself and regulating the chemical changes that take place when becoming triggered or going through trauma.

Personal Rights

In this land of rights, personal rights are anchors to your dreams. One thing I urge you not to do is give up on your dream. If you hold on to your dream, whatever it is, any bad habits you may be doing to ease the pain will eventually subside because your dream will be so big. It will consume all of your time, and you won't have time to waste. But if you do feel like you're slipping into bad habits of drinking and using drugs, then I urge you to do yourself a favor and check yourself into treatment or counseling and tell them your story.

Your Dreams Matter

Your dream has a right to live and to be tested. Give it a shot.

All you can do is try and don't give up on that part! Everybody tells you to go and do it, but maybe all you have to do is take one small step—just one little step toward that dream. If it doesn't feel good, you have every right to pivot, take a different course of action, dream up a new dream, and set a course on a new route.

Researching

Knowing your rights, both personally and legally, is crucial. Here is the Equal Employment Opportunity Commission website: https://www.eeoc.gov/coverage and, more specifically, for businesses: https://www.eeoc.gov/coverage-businessprivate-employers. Being informed about your rights is the first step in advocating for yourself in the face of discrimination.

Check out your city's website to see what ordinances cover you. Don't let tiny things stop you from finding a complaint. Often, if you file a complaint, the city offices must let the employer know that you filed a complaint. You can utilize that as leverage when discussing your separation with them.

Sometimes, the employer will just outright fire you, and there is no discussion and no way to negotiate the terms of separation. In this case, again, it will serve you to file. There might be a process through your city office where they can mitigate those conversations, but they are obligated by law to investigate the complaint. Again, I'm not a legal expert; I want to encourage you to investigate what it takes to file a discrimination case.

Complex Cultura

Despite these challenges, Latinas are incredibly resilient and strong. We are not just sexy, weak, or docile, and certainly not irrationally angry. We are powerful and intelligent, and we have the strength to overcome these obstacles in the workplace.

The problem is that we are not believed in the workforce.

Consider This:

For instance, Latinas often report doing about 20% more office work on average than their white male counterparts, whether it's literal housework, administrative tasks, or emotional labor. This is especially true in high-status high-stakes workplaces. Women engineers report worker bee expectations are higher than those of white men. Women of color reported at higher rates than white women do. Meanwhile, glamor work that leads to new working and promotion opportunities, such as project leadership presentations, disproportionately goes to white men. These are just a few examples of the discrimination Latinas face in the workplace.

And this is in office work—white-collar jobs! Can you imagine a nonprofit world where women, such as teachers, nurses, and social workers, work most of the frontline? What about leadership in a fast-food restaurant, a hotel, or a cleaning company? How does basic respect show up there?

No matter your job, you have a right to work in peace and do your job without fear. Women are already being worked so hard. We are so busy that it only makes sense that we don't have the energy or the stamina to file for a discrimination case.

Historical Context

When it happened to me, the pandemic was just about to begin. I got let go on Martin Luther Junior King Day, January 19th, 2020, and about eight weeks later, the whole world shut down!! In the span of less than 24 months, the World Health Organization (WHO) estimates that approximately 15 million direct or indirect deaths globally from January 2020 – December 2021 that were caused by the COVID-19 pandemic. The world in shutdown gave me pause, but also filled me with anger that people were dying because they were not getting the health care they needed. This situation, exacerbated by the pandemic, highlighted the existing inequalities and discrimination in our society, from the workplace to the healthcare system, and fueled the fight against police brutality and racial discrimination.

In that sadness, we all witnessed George Floyd's murder. I will never forget that image on 38th and Chicago Ave. in South Minneapolis ("George Floyd Square occupied protest," n.d.). I used to ride the metro bus through that neighborhood. I did my undergraduate studies at the University of Minnesota Twin Cities, and I know the store that he went to that day. I know the corner he got killed at. He was murdered intentionally, and the struggle for Black Lives and the end of police brutality is not over.

The whole country came together. We had significant protests that lasted weeks and months, even locally, and there was a 'racial reckoning.' This term refers to a period of time when society as a whole is forced to confront and address the systemic racism that exists. People were fed up with seeing Black folks being killed at the hands of the police. Another example was Tony Robinson (Garton, 2023), who was murdered by a Madison, Wisconsin, police officer for doing what many white college kids do: party. The movement was happening everywhere! I was happy to help distribute masks and connect people with resources through YouTube and FaceBook live actions. I hosted live talks with guests on health, Latina mothering during the pandemic, anti-blackness in the Latino community, local politics, and Latina sexuality.

Racial discrimination and the wealth gap are also part of these protests. People of color worked in areas that were considered essential workers in those days. Code for "you have no choice but to work." They were celebrated, but they also risked their lives, and often, their pay was not in balance with this notion of "essential workers."

Black and Hispanic adults are also more likely to have jobs that are deemed "essential" [8, 9]; these workers (e.g., grocery, food service, retail employees, personal care aides, public transportation drivers, and teachers) are not able to work from home, do not have paid sick days, and are more likely to come in close contact with the public on a daily basis. This invariably increases their risk of exposure to SARS-COV-2, the virus that causes COVID-19 [10]. Zhang and Warner [11] report that in states with higher percentages of marginalized and essential workers, there are higher infection rates, and workers are less likely to receive proper healthcare. (W. Montague Cobb-NMA Health Institute 2023)

Trends and Reality

When we talk about DEI, equality, equity, social justice, or trying to level the playing field, we often do not know what these terms mean or how they are code for a welcoming and safe workplace. What bothers me is that despite these code words, they don't protect us from racial discrimination. Racial discrimination still happens regardless of the declarations of social justice or leadership. As nonprofit workers, we are not protected any better than the essential workers during the pandemic. BIPOC nonprofit folks work long hours for little pay, are harassed into silence, or tokenized to the point that it is harmful.

You are not alone.
I'm not alone.
No estas loca
It's racism.

Every case handled on the federal level is public information, and the settlements are reported, and the costs of racial discrimination are surprising. When looking at the following information, think about the process to get to a court hearing and all that it takes to do a hearing. Many cases are not reported, and we don't have data on cases handled outside of court. We don't know how many times people had the form on their screen tab to do it but never returned to finish the report. Or the number of people who settled for some quick cash called it a wash and kept going back to the very system that hurts and injures not only people but communities.

On a federal level, the number of cases filed has increased. "In FY 2023, the EEOC filed 143 merits lawsuits, 25 of which were systemic, and resolved 98 suits, obtaining over $22.6 million in monetary relief for victims of employment discrimination. The 143 suits represent more than 50% increase compared to FY 2022 levels." When people say that we don't need affirmative action, I would ask them to read the summaries of cases in their district. People get bullied on the job for their hair, for speaking Spanish, for being pregnant, or for having a physical disability. The list goes on.

How do we move on after the tornado of racial discrimination?
Take a beat.
Slow down and feel the season change around you.

I truly appreciate where I live, but our economic system does not work for everyone. Class disparity and racial discrimination are linked. I hope this observation will leave you knowing that no one can take your energy away. Your energy is everything and there will be people to help you.

The Fear

Many people do not file because they fear retaliation. Retaliation happens after you file for discrimination. If you have been retaliated against because you went to human resources and made a complaint, you should also know that you have a right to protect yourself.

Retaliation is another form of discrimination.

Retaliation is when an employer takes adverse action against an employee for engaging in a protected activity, such as filing or making a complaint.

Fun fact: Retaliation is the most frequently alleged form of discrimination in federal cases, per the U.S. Equal Employment Opportunity Commission (EEOC). It is illegal to retaliate against employees or applicants for engaging in protected activities, like filing complaints, discussing discrimination with supervisors, or requesting accommodations. Retaliation can include actions like unfair evaluations, undesirable transfers, or increased scrutiny. While employees aren't shielded from legitimate discipline, employers cannot take actions that would discourage reporting or resisting discrimination. The protection applies as long as the employee reasonably believes workplace discrimination is occurring, even without using legal terminology. (U.S. Equal Employment Opportunity Commission, n.d.).

For more information, Questions and Answers: Enforcement Guidance on Retaliation and Related Issues, visit https://www.eeoc.gov/laws/ guidance/retaliation-qa.cfm.

(EEOC Website, accessed March 2024)

I encourage you to check out the various types of retaliation because I think this is why most Latinas, women of color, and disabled folks often do not file for discrimination because of the fear of reprisals. We know the threat of losing your job is so critical that you would rather stay in line and stay in that crappy job than lose your income. We have been conditioned to tolerate workplace discrimination, and it's become a generational condition that is handed down and molded in our families.

Latinahood in the Workplace

Here is a little poem I wrote about the ways people see Latinas. In it, I go through the phases of being a Latina growing up in a neoliberal Midwestern city.

In elementary school, "She is so cute."
In Middle School, "She is so smart."
In High School, "She has so much potential."
In College, "She is so passionate."
In the workforce, "She is not qualified,"
"Doesn't have the right qualifications,"
"What's that?" (What they say when she says her name)
"She expects too much,"
"Demands too much,"
"She talks too much,"
"Doesn't have a degree,"
"Is too fat,"
"Has a criminal record,"
"Has an accent,"
"Isn't fully bilingual,"
"Can't write in Spanish and wears hot pink lipstick."

That poem came from a phone consultation with another Latina, who was part of a group of Latinas who were pushed out of their nonprofit jobs. We went off about how Latinas are thought of as cute or considered the teacher's pet in school because we excel (I'm witnessing this with my daughter). Still, when we are in the workforce and speak against the systems that keep us barely alive, our sentiments are unwelcome. When we demand a "grown-ass women's wage," these are the sentiments, comments, and underlying messages that we come up against.

Being a poet, married, and having a fabulous, supportive family is how I haven't ended up homeless on the streets, we were homeless in the sense of having to double up with distant family. It wasn't some cake job or a pass; it was my self-resiliency and the generations of other Brown and Black women who came before me and wrote about their struggles. That is how I was able to lift myself out of this depression.

Suddenly, I wasn't alone.

Remember when I told you how I was a community social worker in the early 2000s, assisting many folks with social services and connecting them to resources to help them? You probably can guess I have attended several 'Know Your Rights' and 'How to Advocate for People' seminars.

The Nonprofit Worker Complex

As a nonprofit Social Service provider, you are often inundated with so many types of training. You go, and you're super empowered to help other people, but then it happens to you, and suddenly, it's like all that information just goes out the door. You get freaked out—like a deer in headlights. Remember that friend I told you about who encouraged me to file for discrimination? That lawyer friend from Detroit, Michigan—if she had not told me to file, I don't think I would have done it.

When I was working for the state, I was retaliated against for making a complaint about one of my coworkers who was looking at and engaging with a young brown girl online, and I was so disgusted that I decided to quit on my own. Then, in my last two weeks of work, they retaliated against me and ordered me to leave immediately from the Department. I called our state EOC department to weigh in on the situation. I could have filed; I was encouraged to do so back then, but I didn't. I didn't have evidence of this guy looking at this girl. We (other coworkers knew about this but said nothing) witnessed this bad behavior, and I told HR about it, but it didn't protect me. I did make a stance when I left that day. I marched to HR and told them. It was sneaky that they planted someone to 'tell on me' when I had complained about the new supervisor. Who should you trust on the job? That question gets very complicated when working in the nonprofit industry. Be careful, not only because of your reputation, but for your health.

Boundaries are Beautiful

How do people survive demanding work conditions? What is their secret? I've noticed not to take everything personally, and knowing that the job won't love you back is a helpful reminder. The people who I have seen be successful are people with great boundaries, and even they get burned. It happens everywhere. Workplace safety, board safety, and volunteer safety are things that we don't talk about enough. That day, I chalked it up to "I hate that job anywayz!" And I went back to nonprofit work. Remember, it's not that we don't know what to do. It's about the energy that we have to go through it. Forgive yourself because you are going to have to work again. You will make mistakes again, and you will most likely hear or witness something disrespectful. In order to confront them or challenge the systems that uphold these practices, you need to come from a healed place. Yes, wounded warrior, you will face these challenges again.

I hope you find encouragement y las ganas (deep desire) to use these strategies to heal in any way you need. I find it comforting to know the laws protecting us as a people. I find it comforting to know the reason or psychology behind bias in the workplace and the economic debt it costs us. People have no idea how much money is lost in discrimination suits. But remember, we typically don't report. If we did, what would happen? What could happen?

My Expertise

I teach women and men about uncovering their mission statements because working to help people can give you secondary trauma. Having a mission can help you anchor to the work and understand why you do the work you do. It's important to know why you are doing the work you do. Having a mission statement is meant to help you heal when you are overworked and stressed. Having a vision of the community you want to nurture is necessary to rebuild your career. That is why I'm sharing with you that having a mission statement and incorporating healing activities right now is critical for you to build the career-life and work balance you seek. I wish someone had told me just to collect the unemployment and check myself to a retreat.

Take a Break

During the pandemic, I suddenly found myself wearing a mask and giving away masks downtown. I went from one frying pan to another. Not everyone has the opportunity to take a break from working. My upbringing doesn't let me stop working. It's as if my work is lazy work because I'm not in a field sweating or bent over in a bathroom cleaning. That has been the hardest thing to heal from the skeleton hand telling me that my work is not worth taking a break, or my monkey mind thinking of every possible catastrophic outcome of not working.

North Star

Writing and teaching helped me regain balance in my life and form a community. I love teaching others how to heal through writing and collaboration work. I have found my audiences enjoy the team-building and the freedom to be real. It is empowering to give people the platform and space to talk about their feelings about work and the people they serve.

Healing Activity

▶ Rest, take a break for an hour a day, go outside and walk around, observe how nature speaks to itself, and observe how nature corrects itself.

▶ *Here are some journal writing prompts to use:*
   I remember having Joy in this job when I...
   What is my dream job?
   One thing I love helping people to do is...

Action Strategies

1. Look up your local Legal Aid office's website.

2. Think about your situation as if it wasn't you. "I'm asking for a friend..." what would you say to that friend?

3. Write a timeline of the events six months to a year after you left this job.

Discussion Questions for Groups

1. Is there a local civil rights, disability rights, or equal opportunities commission that you can volunteer for?

2. Where are you in your journey of anti-bias? Is there a destination? (all answers are valid)

3. Does your workplace have the Equal Opportunities Federal poster in the break room?

4. Why is affirmative action looked down upon? Why is it under attack in our nation?

Group activity: Look in the news this week for pieces where affirmative action or equal opportunities have been questioned or attacked. Make it a challenge to find as many cases as possible in seven or fourteen days. Each person should report back to the group.

Ahora Tú: Reflect & Release

CHAPTER 4

GETTING THE HELP
GETTING HEALED

It's not easy to ask for help. We can not heal in isolation. These two powerful and true sentences, often in this busy life, are easy to put aside so that we can continue to work and generate money for life. Let's break down this action of asking for help.

Seeking for legal assistance is intimidating. As a social worker, I have asked for legal help on behalf of many people. They mainly had me do it for them because they felt embarrassed or didn't know how they could articulate the questions. I have found that most legal advisors to the public are caring and understanding people. Asking for legal can be part of your healing journey, but it's NOT required. I'm adding it here because it opens doors for us and can heal an unexpected part of our lives.

What is Legal counsel?

It's a general term for someone who provides legal advice or guidance or represents clients in court. It can also refer to the services or advice provided as part of such representation. Legal counsel or a worker rights advocacy organization can help you make informed decisions in legal matters, including guiding you through complex legal processes, explaining the potential consequences of your actions, and helping you understand your rights and options.

Challenges of Asking for Help

As Latinas, immigrants, and other historically oppressed folks, we are not used to asking for legal help. We think about the cost. Our prior interactions with lawyers can deter us from asking for legal help. Our prior convictions might make us less likely to seek legal counsel. Perhaps we are on probation, or we are an undocumented immigrant. All of these identities can be barriers to seeking legal advice. Even our names can be a barrier; when I ask for help, it begins with a deep breath because spelling out my name day, after day is an act of labor.

Seeking legal help is work. If you Google what to do after workplace harassment, the first suggestion that pops up is to report it. Then it's suggested to document everything. Yes, we must do this, but it is hard to document when you doubt yourself. You will want to share copies of the evidence with the legal help you seek. The list suggests confronting the person, which I would not advise you to do unless you feel safe or get a witness. I can understand why it is suggested we all need to stand up for ourselves at the first sign of smoke. Then, they say to seek legal advice and file a complaint with the EEOC; the last suggestion is to seek support. It's funny because I would say that getting emotional support is the first thing you should do!

Healing and Self-Care

Healing is work, no matter how it may appear from the outside. After experiencing abuse, you deserve rest. Unfortunately, our work life and community often don't make it easy to receive rest or honor our pain. Seeking legal advice can lead to excessive questions about your case, which can be triggering. Discussing how you were treated differently due to any facet of your identity can make you reluctant to share your story. You might even feel angry about it. In these moments, it's crucial to be gentle with yourself, to prioritize your well-being and self-care, and to set boundaries with colleagues and lawyers when discussing your story or case.

Self-care means setting boundaries with colleagues and lawyers when discussing your story or case. Preface the conversation, "This is hard for me to talk about. I can give you a summary or email you more information later."

My book is for women in nonprofit work, because I know that it's exhausting to help others when you are going through some hard times. Talking about your problems can create its own type of fatigue, and it's not uncommon to find yourself physically exhausted every day. It's okay to feel this way, and it's okay to do almost anything to avoid talking about it. I've been there.

Don't be surprised that you are doing almost everything and anything to avoid talking about it.

I know I did.

Before I was let go in January, I had been on a probation freeze for about four months. During this time, I could not talk to them in person. All communication had to go through a chat room, where everyone in the organization would discuss my tasks. A legal outside firm interviewed each employee to determine if there was a substantial case. This freeze time allowed me to collect information and seek different lawyers' opinions, which was a crucial part of my healing journey.

I'm in communications for a reason. I enjoy researching and noticed that I could file my complaint online. Not all cities have complaint forms online as an option, but I'm sure many do. It made it easier for me to file.

Legal Help

Most lawyers will give you a free consultation, but not all. A free consultation might not happen at a time convenient for you. They might say you lack substantial evidence to handle your case. Not having evidence does not impede or prohibit you from filing for Discrimination at your City government website or federal level. Check out free legal aid clinics; talking to a lawyer or legal aid office gives you the advantage of discussing the case without having to file.

Again, I am not a lawyer; this is common knowledge of seeking legal counsel. I encourage you to ask how much it will cost. Ask them if they have experience with discrimination cases in the workplace with nonprofit organizations. Also, you might ask if they know the organization you are bringing up charges against because you don't want them to be biased.

It's Complicated

This is precisely why I didn't go to the legal action offices of my state— our Legal Aid office is also a nonprofit organization and somewhat involved with the organization where I was fired. I had to go outside of my city to ask for help from other lawyers. Most of them told me that it was hearsay. Hearsay is a legal term that refers to information that is not based on the direct knowledge of a person but on what someone else has said. In my case, most of them told me there wasn't any direct, substantial evidence because the abuse she did to me was 1:1, and there were no direct witnesses. Other staff folks did see something, but I think they were afraid to get involved. Since none of what she told me followed up with a direct consequence, such as a pay cut, it was hard to prove the discrimination or harassment.

On this journey, I learned that had I gone to trial, I probably would have settled for more money. I compromised, but I utilized the system to help me. As people of color, as Latinas, we are not taught about how our government can help us. We are told to take it, that it's part of our culture and identity to work and not make ripples. I'm telling you, amiga, it's our civil right, nuestro derecho, to work in an environment free of harassment.

The Impact vs. The Numbers

Had I not become a commissioner for the Opportunities Commission of the City of Madison, I don't think I would've known how much money EOC Chicago offices win in monthly lawsuits. According to my calculations, I received about 1/5 of my salary.

What if I told you that I know many women who go for 1/10 of their salary? I know many women who settle out of court for unfair circumstances like gender discrimination, having a child, or being poor and not being able to afford car repairs. It is hard to find concrete evidence for direct Discrimination. Most of the time, the company will silence you with severance pay. I've counseled many women of color who have quietly left a job for severance pay.

Doing the right thing didn't help me.

In 2019, when I was harassed on the job, I trusted systems. I did the right thing; I called the Human Resources hotline. I made a complaint. I called the employee helpline anonymously, and they gave me suggestions. Suddenly, an outside law firm was contracted, and my supervisor was notified. They interviewed the board and the whole staff, and I fell into a corner. I desperately needed this job for my family and myself. My son was just going to college, and I had just left $18,000 worth of work and gigs. Right before they hired me, I was an entrepreneur and consultant. This organization had been one of my biggest clients.

It felt good to be hired by them.

It was a natural progression.

I was going from that extreme to grieving the passing of my grandmother's death, then going on a lockdown because of a pandemic. It was all very traumatizing and quick.

Latinas and Latinos in the Workforce

I know how Latinas are mistreated in the workforce. I've seen it all of my life in my family life and in society. Nationally, Latinas are over-represented in the restaurant and hospitality industry. As a social service provider, I have witnessed how cleaning companies have not paid their workers or construction companies and are skipping on safety for profit. Consider in 2022 how Latino has the highest fatal injury rate. "According to the Bureau of Labor Statistics, Hispanic or Latino workers had a fatality rate of 4.5 per 100,000 full-time equivalent workers, compared to an overall rate of 3.6. Compared to other workers, a Latino worker is almost 30% more likely to suffer a fatal injury on the job." (RAMOS)

It hurts to know these facts that Latinos are overrepresented in low-paying industries and work in dangerous conditions to provide for their families. Golpes al corazón. I love helping people; it's in my nature, but my grandmother and mother told me about her work conditions, which made me want to go to college. Unreported workplace injuries are prevalent in Latinas' work history, and this happened to mi Abuelita; she bumped her head at a construction site during her University janitorial job, and she had seizures. She was given medical attention but did not receive a settlement; she told me how she believed this injury caused her to lose her sight. My mom was exposed to fumes from the cleaning solutions or radiation from the experiments in the areas where she cleaned. She got hepatitis C and then breast cancer. No one in our family has ever had breast cancer.

I sincerely appreciate folks working on the farms, construction, or demanding labor industries. I have mad respect for them and every work that is done with dignity and honesty.

Not the First Time

My injuries were a mix of emotions and physical reactions to the massive stress the case was causing me. However, because this is not my first time being mistreated in a nonprofit setting, I felt that I needed to move forward in filing with my city agency. The first time that I knowingly experienced racial discrimination in a nonprofit setting occurred in 2016. On that job, as soon as I began to take credit for helping and doing work, I remember this young supervisor yelling at me at the top of her lungs, and then the next day, about how I didn't know about teamwork. The next day, the whole office turned their backs to me as if I were the one who acted irrationally. They were so intimidated by me that they had someone waiting in the hallway, observing the situation of them letting me go. This incident was brutal because we were applying for a house loan then. I needed that job. Thankfully, the following day, I moved into my house. Life has a way of rescuing me, and I love that, and I'm forever grateful.

Only four years later, the same thing happened here, except now I am in a whole new position in the nonprofit field, working in development, and I have been mistreated again. I called for help and used the system this time, but it still didn't work. If my friend hadn't told me what I usually tell people, which is to report it, I wouldn't have reported it. Surround yourself with those good friends who will remind you what to do.

Doing What You Need

If I had sued them; it would've taken years to settle; mi corazón told me it was better to move on. It had already been dragging on for months. Oh my gosh, the last two months were horrible. I remember when they yelled at me when I was just trying to drop off some papers at their office. They made me feel like a coward, like a little mouse.

If I had stayed in that environment, I think it would have cost me more than my self-esteem. In the end, I'm glad I moved on. I've met so many people, so many amazing Latinas at the national level, and so many amazing women, entrepreneurs, and speakers—women I've trained with and women who have taught me! I don't think I would have the life I'm living now if I had stayed there.

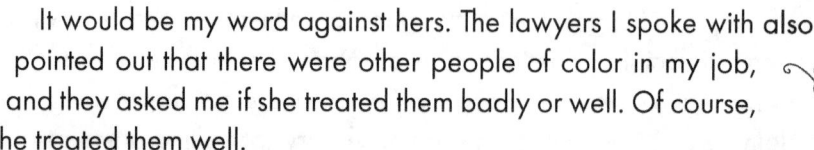

It would be my word against hers. The lawyers I spoke with also pointed out that there were other people of color in my job, and they asked me if she treated them badly or well. Of course, she treated them well.

The Abuse

You see, I was her mark. She had me marked from the beginning. As a survivor of domestic violence and sexual incest, she knew me. She had been following me on social media for years. She idolized me in many ways and praised me for my work. Until she was my direct supervisor, there were no problems between us. The way they showered me with compliments was too sweet. But at the time I simply excused it as friendly.

Then, one day, she told me that she was like the man in the relationship and that, many times, she had trouble working with women. I'll never forget that sunny day, walking my dog and talking on the phone with her, when something inside me stirred. That was my first body warning and another red flag, but I ignored it. I laughed it off and said, "Oh no, are you kidding? It's because we're strong women. I get you." About a year later, I asked myself what kind of "man" she was. Is she the type of man that hurts women?

Reflections and Realizations

As I review the definitions of racial discrimination vs. racial harassment, I'm starting to realize what I suffered was racial harassment. I was racially harassed because of my immigrant background because I am bilingual, and because I'm a woman of color. I was racially harassed because I'm Latina, and I knew this because she would sexualize me in front of others.

You could even say I was harassed because of my sexual orientation for being bisexual leaning. It's not something that I talk about openly, nor do I need to. I'm queer, and living in a het relationship, and they know this. She had talked about how people in her circle thought we were gay in a morning meeting. It was definitely crossing a boundary; she did not ask me permission to share this story about us, and it further shows how she disregarded my personhood. Not appropriate whatsoever, as joke, in a meeting is not cool. Red flag #201.

I think it's crucial for me to talk about this because harassment in the workplace is very nuanced and has many different layers. It's like an onion; each layer has its own particular way of making you cry.

Keep Going

Seeking legal help is hard when you are in the situation and even after you have left the job. These stories are hard to share with a stranger. A lot of people told me I didn't have a case. Maybe they were right, or maybe they were wrong. But that still doesn't take away my right to file for discrimination. That still doesn't take away my right to call out the actions that she did against me as racially motivated and racial harassment. As an empowerment coach for Latinas and a Latina speaker, I talk about healing and how to increase your network. We start with developing your mission statement. The following is a small example of the problem solving that I guide people through. "Guiding" people is my genius area, I excel in helping people and organizations create programs that engages the Latino population.

Here are my suggestions for questions for any legal council you decide to talk to.

Remember to emotionally prepare yourself for answers that are not friendly or empathetic.

▶ What kind of experience do you have with similar cases?

▶ What would be your strategy for my case?

▶ Are there any alternatives to going to court?

▶ What are my possible outcomes?

- Who will handle my case?
- What is my role in my case?
- How much will this cost me?
- How do you communicate with clients?
- Will there be Court filing fees?
- Do you, as a lawyer, have trial experience?

If you choose not to do any of these things, it's okay. It doesn't make you less; it doesn't make you weak not to seek legal counsel. It's your choice. It's your right not to do anything, either.

Straight Talk

Let me take this time to say that there's no Prince Charming here to save you, mujer. Osea, the only person who can help you is yourself. There is great power and opportunity because you can decide how to save yourself. YES! Asking yourself "how" is a great way to shift from victimhood to survivor, to thriver, to a new career or a new life. How are you going to do this? Who can help you?

Healing Activity

- If all you can do for yourself is tell your story to someone else, that's a huge step. If all you can do is write yourself a letter of love or write out what happened and then burn it, it's okay; that's enough.

I know I did.

- Take this time to write some positive statements about the healing you have done to this point.

I'm proud of myself for _____

I helped myself by_____

I know one thing for sure, and that is _____

¡Tiempo de acción time!

Action Strategies

1. Look up three lawyers and try to call them to ask questions about racial discrimination cases; it is essential to know how a lawyer handles a case.

2. Secondly, I wish I had done this myself. Record the conversation if you decide to talk to a lawyer or legal counsel. If you can't record it, write about what you talked about. This action is critical to remembering what they said as advice. *When I would call lawyers, immediately after I hung up, I forgot everything they said to me, including all of their advice. I wish I had recorded it.*

3. Celebrate the fact that you did these first two things. Or celebrate a sunny day or any day that makes you feel good to be alive! Tell someone that you are thriving—that you have hope.

It's time for you to celebrate! Take the time to dive into art, music, or whatever you do to chill. You did a big job and did something para tu futuro!

Discussion Questions for Groups

1. How can you become a community partner for your local civil rights office? Typically, these offices will train your organization or group on filing for Discrimination. It's a Civic action to learn how to file for Discrimination in your community and a perfect way to be an ally.

2. Group Discussion topic: Are ERG groups helpful for employees? Employment Resource Groups have recently become a beacon of hope for diversity and inclusion in the workplace. *If you are a part of an ERG group, have you hosted your own How to File Discrimination in the Workplace workshop? What is holding you back from doing this?*

3. How can you make it safe to talk about identity in your work? I give talks to workplaces and encourage them to talk about their differences. Often, these community centers or organizations

are so engaged in community work that they forget or skim over the very identities of their employees. Challenge your group and talk about it!

Ahora Tú: Reflect & Release

CHAPTER 5

YOU ARE GOLD: BELIEVE YOUR WORTH

Often, we base our self-worth on negative memories, not facts.

Fact: When I got racially harassed, I had three degrees, over 14 years working in nonprofit organizations, contributed to several anthologies, was voted Latina Influencer for Wisconsin, and had a podcast. My abuser told me that I was underqualified for the position. The actions done to me were meant to make me think I didn't have any self-worth.

I remember at my workplace, where the harassment was happening, during a meeting, they publicly humiliated me. They slammed their hands on the desk after I said something. I can't remember exactly what triggered them to do this, except that I remember being in the room by myself after everyone left. I'm not sure how I ended up being alone in the room or why it took me so long to get my things. I'm sure they did this to demonstrate their "superiority" in this meeting.

I blanked out, and it was a way to protect myself for the rest of the day to continue to work, get my kids, get home and cook, welcome my partner, and get to bed; only then did I think about it. At the time, I wished I had been able to report what had happened, but I had normalized the behavior. This was the escalation part, where I think many of us turn a "blind eye" because we believe, "Oh, this is how I belong." Or we justify the action by saying, "They were just joking. This is the culture."

But it's not right.
It's not healthy.

Unfortunately, this behavior is not limited to paid positions. You can find yourself harassed or mistreated because of your identity in volunteer positions.

Community Work Can Be Harmful.

More recently, I was in a board meeting of an organization that I volunteer for, and I was questioned whether I was Indigenous and if I should be the one giving a land acknowledgment. Mind you, my kids both have Nahuatl names (an Indigenous dialect of Mexico). I cried for two days. I didn't confront the woman who did this, nor did I confront the organization's director, who initially had assigned me to do this task. I felt so crushed that no one had stood up for me from this questioning of my identity. I had served on this board for almost two years. I have said the land acknowledgment honoring the Ho-Chuck nation. Although I am not a native of Wisconsin, my people, Mexican people, are native to this continent.

At that moment, I had to do everything to control my anger. I immediately made the subject change to defend the land acknowledgment. Some of them felt it was a meaningless declaration and wanted to change it, but they didn't have another option or plan. They instead thought that coupling me with the women who questioned me publicly would be a smart option to make a sub-committee. Crying that night was my way to fight the depression that could have eaten away at my life. Giving myself permission to mourn is healing. I didn't have time to spare for depression due to a volunteer position.

Healing in Unexpected Places

My solution was to cry and set better boundaries. I decided to end my term, but the next time I decide to join an organization's board, I will investigate their commitment and plan for diversity. Are land acknowledgments meaningless? Maybe, but if you have to question the person's identity giving it, you have bigger biases than what a token board member can ever possibly help with. Setting boundaries is not a sign of weakness, but a powerful tool to protect your worth and well-being. It's a way to take control of your narrative and ensure your voice is heard.

Then, I spent the weekend deweeding my lawn. That was healing, and it made me feel complete. That is what healing does for us; it helps us feel whole through new practices and allows us to create new self-affirmations. Even mourning is healthy. I was mourning the loss of trust I had built with these women just when I was finally getting comfortable. Embracing new practices and self-affirmations can be a powerful tool for healing and growth, offering a sense of hope and inspiration.

Be mindful of what you do after a major episode. Try not to go drinking or engage in any other addictive behavior. Try to rest. Whatever you feel in your heart your body is also experiencing, it's like being near a big boom box speaker at a heavy metal concert— the vibrations going through your body. You will feel wiped out. Drink water.

Being questioned in a meeting about my race was meant to delegitimize my presence in the group. Understanding your worth and living as a survivor is like rebuilding a house over and over again. The stories you tell yourself are fundamental to your identity.

Words matter.

Words will help you grow your worth and build the ideas that are part of who you are, but they're subjective.

That means the words you take from others are subjective about you; they're not based on actual facts. The indisputable truth is that you're a human being, and you're not perfect; nobody is.

It's so important to feed yourself with new perspectives and viewpoints grounded in the present. Try to do better. No one is a saint. Who you are right now matters. If you continue to carry yourself in what you were doing or how you reacted when initially discriminated against, you will stay there. Reliving those moments and shaming yourself for not speaking up is not healing. Let go of self-criticism and focus on the present to feel liberated and at peace. Embrace the present moment, and let it guide you towards peace and acceptance.

Living in an angry place is not helpful for anyone.

La Toxica.

Many people have been using this word on social media, and it's funny. It's a term in Latino culture to define someone (so men can be toxico too!) with toxic traits, like being overly jealous, possessive, and dramatic when it comes to their partner. Yes, I can be that person, too, but I can also move past that or utilize those things that made me toxic for a purpose. I can turn my pain into passion or into whatever I want. The choice is mine. People may think oh, you are complaining about small stuff, but when you think about how much money is paid for discrimination cases, it's more than just being overly sensitive or dramatic. Workplace abuse is painful and can led to persistent conditions of imposter syndrom, depression, and anxiety, people pleasing, and squishy boundaries for work.

Your Worth and the dangers of Imposter Syndrome

Knowing your worth is important because it can motivate others to care for themselves and explore their full potential. Knowing your worth is vital for your potential earning power and will help you pivot after you leave or if you have been fired from your job. Imposter syndrome, is a real condition, but I also believe it's a condition that is brought on because of how society treats Latinas and Black women in the workplace and in general.

What is the difference from having low self-esteem to imposter syndrome? Low self-esteem is the idea that you lack a general ability to succeed. Impostor syndrome comes from the imbalance between strong knowledge (lived, earned or from schooling) and what you *should* be capable of doing, and then comparing it to one's own lack of practical experience. It's like being a doctor and not being able to speak up at a meeting that you know you have the credentials and expertise to speak on the subject.

I have both. I got low esteem from the abuse in my early childhood and then regardless of my education and personal knowledge, I wasn't valued, that gave me impostor syndrome. What I don't like about this term is that it doesn't tell the full story of how imposter syndrome can come from racial and gender inequalities and you feel like it's confirmed when faced with low wages, or persistent job losses. Another thing I don't like about this term is that it's used for professional workplaces, but I think imposter syndrom happens in all workplaces for all people who work. You can be an administrative assistant, a nurse, teacher, mechanic, sales clerk and still feel that you don't have the worth to ask for a raise or be promoted or not be skilled to move up or move to a new industry because of imposter syndrome that comes from working in a place or places that have not valued you.

Remember to breathe in and breathe out. Healing is work.

Healing Break

Visualize a moment when someone witnessed that one thing that you're good at.
Think about how you made them feel.
Think about how you feel when you are finished doing this work.
Really put yourself in that moment.
What does it look like?
What does it feel like?
What are the colors of the walls?

Are you inside?

Are you outside of an office?

Are you in nature?

Are you helping somebody in the hospital?

Where are you when you are doing this one thing you're good at?

Visualizing yourself doing the work you love will help you pivot and rewrite a narrative that is grounded in your good work.

Evidence of Our Discrimination

I referenced this book in a previous chapter, but for this chapter, it's worth reviewing and diving deeper. The Historian as Curandera by Aurora Levins Morales discusses making absences visible in our history. When investigating and telling the history of disenfranchised people, you can't always find the kind and amount of written material you want. However, in medicinal history, the goal is as much to generate questions and show inconsistencies as it is to document people's lives. For example, tracing absences can balance a picture, even when you cannot fill in the blanks (Levins Morales, 1997).

She says that tracing the outlines of a women-shaped hole in our human records and talking about the existence of women about whom we know only general information can be a powerful way of correcting imperialist history (Levins Morales, 1997). I speak in great detail about my grandmother and her journey as an immigrant because I am making it known that her experience is part of our history in Wisconsin. Mi Abuelita was a state worker who faced discrimination on the job and contributed to our society. As a Mexicana living in Wisconsin, through storytelling, I'm correcting the idea that only white people live in Wisconsin. Now, we have several books about Latinos and Black folks in Wisconsin. My story, her story, and your story are the threads that make up our new United States history.

The lack of evidence doesn't mean you can't name and describe what is missing. REPEAT this phrase!

The lack of evidence doesn't mean you can't name and describe what is missing or what happened.

Before we approach this next writing moment, I want you to dig into the landscapes of your life. Make yourself the site of experimentation and engage with how you are represented in this country's history of workforce development. This practice will help you understand your worth.

If you had to use a metaphor for the work you do, what would it be?

Use your surroundings: street, farms, trees, land, buildings, gutters, backyard, lamppost, lakeshore, or a BBQ. Describing your setting is your secret weapon; it's the one place that workplace discrimination can't take away from you. You have your home and all the places that you frequent. Write about this place and your place in this landscape.

Write about how you see yourself giving help. Are you a river or a rock? Are you a flower? If so, what is your function? Why did you choose this?

"A woman who writes has power, and a woman with power is feared."
--Gloria E. Anzaldúa (Anzaldua)

I wrote about redefining my worth in the anthology *of Hispanic Life*. In this essay, I discuss how I had to change the way I saw myself as a leader:

Being a creative individual comes with many strengths. We are natural connectors, visionaries, and innovators. We see the big picture, but often, we second-guess ourselves because we connect the dots effortlessly.

As women of color and first-generation college graduates, we walk through the world with a vulnerability that makes our journey engaging and human. This vulnerability is also our weakness. We give away our ideas with hope and not a business contract. In our vulnerabilities, we get into unproductive negativity that drives people away when we need people to help us.

In my journey to discovering my brand and business, I tried many different hats. I tried the "yes" hat because saying yes to everything helps gain the right connections, right? I tried the consultant hat and gave input to the planning and implementing programs and projects. I was like Yoda, but not getting that Hollywood recognition. Volunteer work does pay off, but make sure it aligns with your goals and career. I tried the Mommy/PTO leader hat, but while I love our school, the lack of diversity in the PTO impacted me. I tried all these hats but left my hat on the hook.

Because I didn't believe I was enough. When other people told me I was enough, I would look into their eyes and run in fear. Fear is the last bridge you want to cross.

As Latinas or Chicanas, we are taught to give to our *familia*, to our husbands, and to our children before giving to ourselves. I still get teary when I leave my house, husband, and kids behind. I somehow shake off that old Mexican hat for this Business Mujer hat, which is who I am. The Wisconsin woman who spends her days discovering her boundaries, anchoring her goals on firm ground. In my vulnerable moments, I discovered my brand was a Mexican export but cultivated with a Midwest point of view for outreach, marketing, and social media strategies that come from a unique place of resilience, radical self-love, and cultural awareness. As Gloria E. Anzaldúa says, "A woman who writes has power, and a woman with power is feared."

Midwest Mujeres is the organization that I founded in 2019. We help women of color tell their stories on stage, much like how I have navigated through restoring myself, and now I help others do it well. (www.midwestmujeres.com)

I leave you with this: follow *mujeres* who see the horizon of our society's ills, who work daily to undo the historical oppressions that we face in the U.S. Don't dismiss *mujeres* who are de casa, o the muy muy independant, the salt of the earth women. You can learn so much from their commitments to their families or communities. You will need to learn how to do your business, and there is no magic, quick way to get ahead. It takes work, both inner and outer work. Focus on your message, what you want for yourself, and exactly who your audience is. There will be bad days, but remember you are not alone (Edelman, 2020).

Healing Activity

Only do breathwork and journaling if it's helpful. Sometimes, it can be too intense and make trauma worse. Get support when you need it.

This healing practice of a body scan is meant to get you out of your head and into your body. You can practice body scan meditation whenever you feel stressed or several times throughout the day. In my experience, it was about going inward. My grandma was very religious and spiritual, so often, it was in prayer that I would allow myself to connect to my body. I would feel that release and let go of my shoulders and temples. Meditation, praying, or sitting in silence in your car or at home and emptying out, is a powerful way to reset and set up for a powerful day. If you have access to massage, myofascial release, or craniosacral therapy, I highly recommend it. Reiki, swimming, and laying on the grass are also great ways to get into your body, where the rest of the healing will need to take place.

Body Scan Time!

1. Get comfortable. You can perform a body scan in any setting, even on the go, but when you're just learning how, you may want to start by sitting or lying down.

2. Close your eyes. If you're uncomfortable closing your eyes, drop your gaze downward so you're not distracted by anything around you.

3. Begin with a few deep breaths. Breathe slowly in through your nose and out through your mouth. Let go of your shoulders and settle into your hips.

4. Start at the top of your body. Focus on your head, asking yourself what sensations you feel in this part of your body. This is super important: Don't judge yourself or judge if you feel tension.

5. Move down your body. Turn your attention down to your shoulders and upper back. Feel where it's tight and send loving vibes, do not judge yourself if you are only able to do your head, butt, and feet. There is no perfect way to do this.

6. Focus on your mid-body. Notice what you feel in those areas when you mentally move down to your chest and belly. If you're sitting in a chair, pay attention to the sensation of your body in the chair; if you're lying down, notice the feeling of your back on the floor or bed.

7. Continue the process down your body.

8. Finish at your feet. Finish your body scan by scanning down to your feet and toes, bringing awareness to those areas of the body and how they feel.

9. End the process gently. Slowly bring your attention back to your surroundings, take a slow, deep breath, and gently open your eyes (Young, 2023).

Soul Work

Mami, Mujercita, Nena, Carino, Love Yourself!

When you love yourself, you understand your values and realize your time is valuable. You can spend this time doing things that you love. It also gives you the confidence to stand your ground while responding to others firmly. Loving yourself is evident in everything you do, from walking to talking to living.

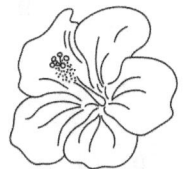

Why is self reflection difficult?

Reflection requires us, as Curanderas (healers), to begin with a practice that ends with digging into your chest and pulling out your heart. Reflection means looking at your heart as an abstraction— from merely an organ to an icon symbolizing love. Reflection means sitting with your dreams, guilt, the tiny ideas that have shaped who you are, and the memories you have chosen to lock up and forget. Reflection is also about letting go. For me, it was about crying near the grave of my Abuelita and asking her for forgiveness.

Is there a specific process?

No, there isn't. It's a constant process. It's a circular spiral pattern, a hole that you walk into, and if you see it again, you walk around it. You see this hole the third and fourth time and react and act differently each time. Each solution is a resolution to a new discovery.

To know our worth, we also need to understand that there are stories we have accepted as our own when, in fact, they are not. These voices of failure or "not enough" are what we believe others have us. The Monkey mind will jump to the conclusion and assumption. The skeleton hand tells us we are not enough. Every story has a creepy shadow that lurches in the background.

Fear and the critical voice

Things that keep me in fear:
If I show my true creativity—
I'll be considered crazy.
Who do you think you are to dream so big?
Well, that's not a good idea.
This is the voice of self-doubt, a self-prophecy of fear, failure, and division.

Don't let doubt and self criticism steal your story.

Tu gente will honor your stories.
A new story, your new story starts with an inhale
Your story rests in your body, like your breath
The satisfaction of completion ends at exhalation
That gives you a smile, a chuckle, a restful night.
Nuestros cuentos are the antidote for fear.

Action Strategies

1. Set boundaries: When you respect yourself, you can extend that compassion to others. For example, you can learn to say no, which can help people respect you.

2. Be aware of your strengths. Sometimes, as Latinas, we don't talk about our strengths. We only talk about our strengths in relation to what we can do for others.

   For example, "I'm a great mother because my family likes my cooking." It's great that they like it, but how about, "I help my family feel connected to new foods because of my unique taste for opposing flavors that I use when I cook."

   Notice the change and ownership and how it brings out your expertise.

3. Write or define your values. Your values help you determine who you are and what matters to you. For example, if you value transparency, you might want every association you have with other people to be honest.

Discussion Questions for Groups

When investigating and telling the history of disenfranchised people, you can't always find the kind and amount of written material you want.

1. Many of us make absences visible in our work. How do we find the evidence of our work and the importance of our location?

2. Find yourself in the landscape of the work that you love to do.

For example, finish the sentence, "I help move earth to make way...."

Extra Discussion Topics for Individuals or Groups

Could you leave your job today?

Is your purpose to make a system of work that only depends on you, or are you building something that others can take over if you leave?

Who are you mentoring at your job or in your community?

Ahora Tú: Reflect & Release

CHAPTER 6

TAKE THE LEAP

Take the leap. What does it mean? It is about acknowledging the pain that workplace discrimination has caused you and deciding not to measure yourself against that failure. It means believing in the hope of better days.

There's a book called *Taking the Leap* by Greg Hendricks. He gives us pointers on overcoming our fears and learning to live happier lives. Confidence is what workplace harassment or discrimination takes from us, and it steals our joy to work for people, our communidad y familias. We begin to believe what racism tells us: that we are not worthy. One thing I enjoyed about the book was how Hendricks talked about working in our *zone of genius*. I think that healing can help us work in our zone of genius. By taking stock of the abuse that we went through, we can begin to own our expertise and experience as rich areas of validation.

Leaping is healing. As the saying goes, "What can you possibly lose that they haven't already tried to take?" This is a question we ask ourselves when we are in that pivotal moment of either releasing our voice or taking the leap of faith in an action that could even sacrifice our lives or safety. I know I've been in many protests and moments where I could have been arrested or harmed because I was standing up for my right to exist.

What I will tell you is that win or lose, you've already won because you are right here, right now, reading this book. You are not alone.

You are Loved.

You are already on the right path to figuring out your life after being fired because of racial discrimination or any other type of discrimination in the workplace.

You are invaluable as a worker. Your unique skills, experiences, and perspectives contribute to the richness of your workplace. Your worth is not determined by the discriminatory actions of others. You are a valuable asset to any team.

Your work is not just valuable; it is essential. Your contributions, no matter how big or small, make a difference. Your worth is not defined by the discrimination you've faced. You are a valuable worker and your work matters.

You are worthy to have a workplace where you are respected and treated with dignity and care, and your opinions matter. You have the right to be paid a living wage with healthcare benefits and a retirement package. You have a right to work where your miles will be reimbursed at the same state rate as everybody else's. You have a right to work in a place where you don't have to fear that your sexual orientation or gender is centralized or sexualized for the entertainment of others. You have a right to work for yourself if that's your choice. You have a right to work in a non-profit organization again and again if that's what you decide to do. You have a right to work for a business workplace if that's what you choose to do.

Not Alone

I felt ashamed that I was let go. I felt incompetent. I mean, heck, they even said I was incompetent and that I wasn't qualified enough for the job that I had. Everyone has felt incompetent regardless of their employment or education. Consider this statistic of STEM professionals experiencing sexual harassment in 2022.

Nearly two-thirds—62%—of women working in science, technology, engineering, and mathematics (STEM) professions claim they've experienced workplace sexual harassment, and a 54% majority alleged they were subjected to multiple instances of harassment at various jobs throughout their careers (DiDio, 2022).

Again, you're not alone, and being fired due to workplace discrimination is not an indicator of your intelligence, strength, or how good you are at your job. I'm not saying that perhaps you weren't doing something wrong in another way, but that doesn't excuse them from utilizing your identity to get back at you. It simply means that they're a lousy manager. They have no fundamental skills in management, and they don't know how to be direct without being abusive. They would rather abuse you than try to encourage you to correct yourself.

Why Filing is Healing

Here is why filing for discrimination is essential. Had I not filed, I guarantee they would have offered me $1,000. Instead, I walked away with about 10 times more. Many women I have spoken to who haven't filed for discrimination are given much less because that's all they can do at that time—they don't have the fight in them to go farther, and that's okay! At least they brought it up, and at least they got something. They took the leap, and they tried. All you can do is try.

This healing/Curandera work is not about revenge. Since the harassment, I've gone to a couple of events with this person who discriminated against me and harassed me. They simply don't have the power to make me mad anymore. People have asked me what I do when I see them. I look right through them as if I see nothing. For those of us working in the non-profit industry, I'm sure you know what I'm talking about.

Rising Above

We say we are about community, yet we are invited to events where the people who have harmed us are right there. We don't say anything for fear of upsetting the people who support us. I know that was my case because I am now a founder of an organization. That work that she said I wasn't good enough at, I flipped it on its head and took the leap. We are a small organization con corazón!

I won't allow another person to steal my joy and talents and prevent me from helping the next person reveal theirs. My work and your work are too important in this world to allow someone else's hate to get in the way of helping someone else.

How can you leap into healing? By practicing soul work.

Soul Work

Every day, we witness the rituals of our planet: sunrise and sunset, night and day, birth, growth, and death. Rituals for hibernation, storing food and water, and making a nest in nature serve a purpose. Rituals for your soul are actions that, on the surface, might not seem to be a big deal. Rituals serve a magical and healing purpose. Rituals open, celebrate, or close an event. Rituals can be tiny moments, where I can ask myself:

What am I doing to help my soul rest, reflect, and refuel? They are simple, tiny movements that I have found useful. I simply ask myself: What am I doing to help my soul rest, reflect, and refuel?

Make a mental list of what things you did today for self-love. Self-love, in this book, means doing anything that helps you feel better, whether it's cooking, sitting in silence, paying rent, going for a walk, going on a quiet bus ride, applying fancy lotion, going to see a movie, etc. For 30 seconds,

think of how you do self-love actions—what do you do for self-love?

When I train women for storytelling, I tell them to think about the one thing they want to leave their audience with. And that's what I want to say to you right now: You have a gift, and you were called to do this type of heart-led work in our community.

You are capable of being an advocate, a bilingual social worker, a connector, a housing specialist, a medical assistant, a medical advocate, a child care provider, a grant writer, a community organizer, an outreach specialist, a development director, or whatever your title is. You were called to do this work in this industry. Just because you met the wrong person doesn't mean you should allow them to sour the work you were put on this earth to do.

Focus on the people you've helped.
Focus on the community that you love.
Focus on the culture that you come from.

Focus on the love you have created and the community you have impacted. It means something, and no one else can do exactly what you do. I don't care if they go and hire somebody else right after you. I don't care if they can help 100 more people than you. No one can help people the way you do. You have a unique style and way of helping people. Take the leap and value yourself.

I have listened to many Mujeres talk about how they overcame self-doubt and how they radically loved themselves. Why is it so hard to think about loving ourselves? I'm talking about building your confidence by looking at each time you had to start over and learn from what you did to survive. In each client session, I have noticed myself creating strategies and discussing social justice with expertise and confidence. When I began using my lived experience as a fountain of wealth, I saw changes in the business opportunities

that were coming my way. I am the Queen of starting over!

The more people I met, the more comfortable I was attracting, NOT Chasing my circle of support, community, and work.

I repeat: It took confidence and self-love to attract my ideal clients, not chase them!

This time, I wasn't just starting over. I was building a brand with a community of women—Mujeres. Hence, the birth of Wisconsin Mujer and later Midwest Mujeres. I want to build a community of women who want to grow their incomes, celebrate their skills, and define their money mindset so that when tragedy does hit, we are better prepared, networked, and able to share our stories so others can grow.

Tragedies

In 2011, my family and I survived a major robbery and homelessness, but through it, we confidence in ourselves that can not be taken away. When we were robbed, I didn't set out to become wealthy, but now I want to become rich, and I am confident I will succeed. Continuing my education, asking for help, and cultivating confidence in my brand are all parts of my money mindset.

Out of tragedy, flowers can grow.
New ideas can be realized.
Take the leap to declare your worth and wealth.

Resiliency has helped me pursue bigger projects and broader horizons. Becoming a speaker and leader was not easy, but I love what I do; I love highlighting movements done by other Black and Brown social entrepreneurs,

and sharing what I have learned brings me great joy!

Starting over this time isn't just for me; I want it for everyone. I'm sharing my story with you so you can all have the space and community to help you take that leap. Starting over is excellent! Making money is also great, but building your confidence is more; it's priceless!

Healing Activity:

▶ Take some time to write and heal. Light some incense, maybe pour a glass of Jamaica (or your favorite beverage), and write. End the following phrases.

My dream job is…
My work is in alignment with…
I like to help others by…

Action Strategies

1. Make a vision board! Get a bunch of magazines and create a vision board of the type of workplace you want. Cut out words that describe the kind of work you want to do. Describe the place and how you want to be treated there. What does this workplace look like and feel like? I have found it useful to make vision boards on Canva. It's a funky, free graphic design application that is super user-friendly.

2. Find a mentor. Go network, get out of your house, and meet people. I know it's hard. They're going to ask you what you do. Feel free to use this framework: "Hello! How are you? Good to hear! I'm doing well. I'm here to connect with people because I'm seeking new opportunities in X area. I love helping people do x, y, and z." Notice, you don't need to say I was fired. Keep it simple and authentic.

3. If you are looking to pivot, meaning you're looking for a different position in the industry—say you're moving from outreach co-ordinator to donor specialist—go check out an association that deals with becoming a donor specialist in the non-profit area. That would be AFP, the Association of Fundraising Professionals. Research the next career move you're going to make.

When networking, remember you don't have to tell everybody everything because you need to have boundaries. That's private; they don't need to know everything.

Discussion Questions for Groups

1. Does everyone who takes a leap start from the same place?

2. How can we encourage people to take a leap?

3. Talk about the times you took a leap of faith and what you learned about yourself.

Ahora Tú: Reflect & Release

CHAPTER 7

FREE YOUR VOICE

What does it mean to free your voice? Sometimes, to free your voice, you must look at it from the very bottom. It means different things at different times in your life. It's a transformational time in your life when you live life without worry and are practicing peace. Seeking mindfulness moments can help us silence the negativity and listen to who we really are. I had to go back to Mexico, where my uncle and abuelitas had passed away and where my childhood abuser lives. Then I went to Guatemala to find peace writing between the mountains, then back to the island of my college town. All of this traveling was to help me finish this book. Helping other people and helping my family gave me the confidence to finish my book. In Mexico, I helped my mom and cousin by just being family. In Guatemala, I consulted several entrepreneurs on their dreams and journey.

For me, it was summoning the courage to talk openly about the racial harassment that I encountered at a nonprofit organization. When I was in my late 20s, on the brink of my marriage, it meant sharing with my partner about the trauma of rape and incest I had endured. And as a young child, at the tender age of nine, it meant finding the bravery to run to my neighbor's place and call the police to save my mother from a life-threatening situation.

Freeing your voice is either a reaction or an action against the cage that oppression or abuse that wants us to be kept in. You don't have to be loud, but you can if you want to. You can raise your hand and talk. A free voice is a light burden. It gets heavy when we don't speak about our dreams, passions, or who or where we came from.

Reinventing

After the workplace incident, I made a conscious decision to harness the power of storytelling. By speaking out about racial discrimination in a course or as a social justice issue, I was able to connect with a community who shared similar experiences of isolation and abuse in their jobs. Now, I empower other women to share their stories. Storytelling is not just a craft, it's an art, and it's your skills plus your secret sauce. Every woman and person has a unique way of telling a story. I love teaching women about the lessons I learned during the pandemic. It was during this time that I met wonderful speaking and storytelling coaches. I learned that freeing your voice can build confidence in closing the wage gap.

I found that freeing your story, voice, and experiences is necessary to close any gap in your life. Positive self-talk is uncommon for first-generation Latinas; we don't have a wide set of positive stories we tell ourselves. Do I think it works? Yes. Do I use positive self-talk to smooth over my B.S.? NO!

When I started this book, I told you, I was crying in an elevator because I was about to jump this person. Freeing your voice also exposes our shortcomings and lessons learned in a clenched smile or at the end of a deep exhalation of exhaustion. It's about when you are about to give up and something pulls your morals, faith, or values.

Methods

I draw from the circular nature of Indigenous storytelling and teach the women how to use metaphor and magical realism in their stories. Like in my story, mi Abuelita ghost guides me to my true nature. In my narration, it's not as long as a book, but the beginning is the story's context. I made a choice that was meant to serve not only my community but to save my dignity. Freeing your voice could also mean telling someone your story or privately recording it on your phone and not sharing it.

For a year after the incident, I would record myself or write only one sentence at a time about what happened to me. It was painful to talk about and to be in a community with my peers, who saw me try and try again to fall and fail. I put a lot of pressure on myself. I'm glad that I was able to find guides who told me what I needed to see: this was an opportunity!

Tu Poder es tu Voz, Your Power is Your Story!

Many of us fail to tap into or fully utilize the true power of our voice. To step into more of our power, we must start by examining what's holding us back. We all engage in negative self-talk about so many things every day, most of which are untrue. What are the stories that you are telling yourself about your voice? It's crucial to reflect on these narratives and understand how they shape our perception of our voice.

That skeleton hand will tell you...
You sound dumb
You sound like you are not educated
You sound fake

The Power of Stories

All our stories can be categorized as stories about our past, future, or both. The most powerful force in the world is the ability to tell stories. All behavioral change happens subconsciously. Stories bypass the conscious mind and cut straight into the subconscious, influencing the listener to learn the lessons taught and take action accordingly. The best leaders are the greatest communicators because they can inspire others to take action by telling stories.

Your story is your greatest asset to getting the job or career you want. Learn to tell your story in a way that relates to your listener. The key to accessing the most powerful version of our voice is identifying these stories that illustrate your passion and dedication and slowly writing or talking about those moments.

Freeing your voice can manifest in many ways, from positive to negative, and you can call out all of the negatives in your life and stand down each of them. We hear this tradition in hip hop songs; no matter what approach, this action can help you win or conquer your fears. Track and field legend Carl Lewis once said, "My thoughts before a big race are usually pretty simple. I tell myself: Get out of the blocks, run your race, stay relaxed. If you run your race, you'll win ... Channel your energy. Focus." It worked for Lewis, who won nine Olympic gold medals and one silver.

Before I started this book, I wrote this essay about what happened to me in 2019. I want you to hear the conviction and struggle, but also the positive slapback in each sentence. Positive speaking isn't linear. In my essay, that sparked this book is a call and response to the skeleton hand voices of negativity with hope.

Here Is My Free voice:

In February 2019, I found myself crying in an elevator because I was about to jump a woman at a party who had fired me. I was furious because I had spent twenty years of hard work in the nonprofit sector, coupled with my education, and because of the racial harassment of this woman, I doubted my worth. I thought for a split second that my integrity was worth less than this moment. Grateful for mi Abueltia and her protection over me that night. How could I give this woman the power to topple over what I believed was the pinnacle of my career? This crushing emotional blow of racial discrimination and harassment engulfed me in rage.

As a forty-year-old Latina facing the aftermath of being fired, I stood at a crossroads. Would I succumb to despair, drown my sorrows in drugs, or numb the pain with alcohol? Or would I dig deep, reconnect with my roots in social justice, and reignite the fire that initially propelled me into community activism?

I had to make a choice that wasn't easy. I went to therapy. The pandemic had us in a complete shutdown. As the world got quiet, I did too. I chose to reclaim my mission, reaffirm my commitment to fighting for justice, and honor the journey that had brought me here. Despite the setback, I refused to let discrimination define me. Instead, I would let it fuel my determination to create a more equitable world. I was armed with the resilience of my heritage and the unwavering conviction that change was not just possible but necessary.

I was done being unfulfilled and undervalued in the nonprofit industry for my work. Unlike being a single parent or a first-generation college student, I had nothing to lose this time. I began believing in myself and created a network to empower other Latinas and women—because I knew I wasn't alone.

Latinas often leave their jobs and are passed up for promotions or are bullied out of their jobs. In the job market, I am sadly reminded how Latinas, regardless of education, only make .55 cents to the dollar earned by a white man. The gender pay gap is even worse for Latinas with college degrees.

As a community social worker, I'd heard the stories of being bullied on the job, of being harassed, or of being silenced for years. I knew I wasn't alone in feeling like this world had no space for me. I knew I wasn't alone in feeling like my education didn't serve me in my career when facing the discrimination or bias of my first name. I wasn't alone in earning .55 to the dollar of a typical salary. This time, instead of settling, I took all of the strategies and my great ideas and started a network for women passionate about their community and social justice and making an impact.

I chose to be that role model I didn't have as a young adult. I began to believe in the movement to break the isolation of Latinas living in the Midwest, but this was different from the other work I'd done. This time, it would be bold, and this time, it would be about culture, social justice, and economic self-empowerment. With George Floyd's murder, it was a calling that I could not put aside because of my imposter syndrome or other fears.

I was ready to do the work to leave a legacy as mi Abuelita had been over six decades ago when she migrated to Wisconsin from Mexico. For years, as a migrant worker, she picked vegetables up and down the Midwest and one day decided to make Wisconsin her home. I, too, decided to stop running, stop settling, and create a new digital home where Latina voices from the Midwest would be valued and honored.

I was tired of being the token Latina in the community for pictures and money but then ignored by decision-makers when I spoke of empowerment for Latinas. I was tired of going to strategy meetings and still having to go to a pantry after talking about how to combat poverty in my community. Fed up with having an education and having nothing to show for it while being in debt up to my ears.

Back then, I didn't know about the wage gap, specifically, but I had always known what it felt like to live it. And now I know what to do about it. From education to hiring practices, I was behind. I had untreated dyslexia, and my name was and is a huge barrier to getting a job. People assumed that I wasn't a U.S. citizen, that I didn't speak English, or that I wasn't born in Wisconsin. I was the pink flamingo in the white snowland of El Norte!

What has enabled me to be resilient and persistent in my dreams is my love for my culture and community. For every heartbreak, disappointment, and dollar I lost, my culture and community have been there to uplift and empower me with ganas and desire—a desire and commitment to continue my grandmother's legacy that began in 1924 when she crossed the border at six months old.

For years, I didn't believe I could make an impact or lead it. I felt that I needed permission, a certain type of education, or to be a part of some crowd to fulfill my dreams. In the end, after my career crashed, although I felt I had nothing, I had my online community! With Midwest Mujeres (the organization and platform that I founded and helped build) as my sounding board, I defined my mission to serve my community by creating a platform for women to elevate their voices and create a digital presence that could help us get better-paying jobs. Closing the wage gap is everyone's responsibility. I have found that teaching mujeres how to tell their stories is the game changer.

Storytelling is a way we can close the wage gap.

That, my friends, is my free voice.

My Mission

It's my heart's desire to help other women free their voices in the same way women have helped me free my voice. It's part of healing the world; it's part of us, and each of you reading this right now has the power to help someone else free their voice, too. You're the reason I just wrote all of this; you're the reason I'm writing this right now.

Workplace discrimination is the twin sibling of the wage gap. One is a systematic symptom of the other, and the wage gap exists because of workplace discrimination. This discrimination helps perpetuate wage gaps and keeps it alive and well. That is why I created my organization, Midwest Mujeres. In our group sessions, I teach Latinas and Black women the fundamentals of storytelling. We teach the women how to tell their stories, and the women go on theatrical stage and talk about why they want more money and what they have done to have fulfilling lives despite the wage gap.

Some people might think we are whining about what we don't have, that we haven't tried hard enough to get equal pay for our work, or that we are to blame for earning less. Our level of production puts all of these voices to rest. We work to deliver a masterpiece of empowerment and transformation. Each story comes with a lesson of hope and self-discovery; the women in our program leave us with a specific call to action for the audience each year. Watch here: https://bit.ly/yoquierodinero24

The irony is that in this country, we protect people who systematically don't pay their workers enough. Our society praises successful business owners who know the system, and we congratulate them for making hundreds and thousands of dollars on the backs of low-paid wage workers, most of whom are people of color.

The Challenge

This whole book is about what you and I can do despite this racist rat race. We can unify ourselves. We can form a human ladder and crawl our way out of this cage. I might be a rat, and I might be Brown, but I'm not ignorant anymore of how this rat race is rigged against us. We have been fooled that we are each other's competition and enemy when, in fact, there's a lot more cheese out there. There are a lot more places out there where there's free cheese. (Sorry, I'm a picture book writer who happens to be from Wisconsin, so you've got to forgive my analogy of mice and cheese. I can't apologize for my love of cheese, though.)

Yes, I'm being completely real about our superpowers. Frequently, this system has us believing that we are powerless and that the only way to get to the cheese is by going through the maze. Free your voice, and you will have a new perspective. You will have a new map that will show you where there's more cheese. You have to trust that everything inside you already knows what to do. Of course, you've made mistakes. I have made tons of mistakes throughout this whole process. Mistakes are okay.

Today, I stand before you to remind us of a profound truth: the goal is not merely to stop at justice. Justice is crucial, yes, but it is not the final destination. It is a milestone on a much longer, more arduous journey.

The ultimate goal is liberation.

Liberation is definitely about legal rights or policy changes—and it also means the total freedom for all people to exist fully and authentically in their own bodies, free from fear and oppression. That part.

Like I'm tired. Of people being killed. Everyday. Everyone is. Gun control. Is liberation. For me liberation means living in a world where no one's **identity, faith, orientation, or abilities are policed or questioned**. Imagine a world where you don't have to justify your existence and can simply be—without the weight of judgment or the burden of stereotypes. I"m tried of being the token, we all are and yet we still do it. This is the world we are striving to create. How do we get there?

Liberation alone is not enough. We must demand action. But many of us need Healing.

Healing from centuries of trauma, from the wounds inflicted by systems that have sought to dehumanize and diminish us. We are healing from the pain of being told that we are less than, not enough, or somehow unworthy of respect. And then they want to take away your dignity.

No Te Dejes.

Don't allow it. Get real about boundaries, and friends. Healing is a process, and it's not something we can do alone. It requires community, and friends, and family both chosen and blood. Give YOU big amounts of compassion, and the courage to confront our past while you build a better future. Healing is about reclaiming nuestra historias, casas, and our corazones. It's about transforming este pinche dolor into power and wounds into wisdom.

And the prize, my friends, is joy.

Joy is a radical act. In a world that so often tries to strip us of our happiness, reclaiming joy is an act of defiance. It's about celebrating who we are, where we come from, and where we are going. Joy is about finding light in the darkest of times. Laughing at someone's funeral and drinking is the most Mexican thing we do. And I love it. Joy is what fuels us on this journey. It's what reminds us why we fight, why we persevere, and why we refuse to give up. It's not enough to survive; we must thrive.

We must reclaim the joy that has been denied to us by the media, by La Migra, by schools that refuse to teach our children and police and ICE that pick up our families.

We need to celebrate and share our joy in this journey to liberation.
Joy in our cultures.
Joy in our communities.
Joy in our sonrisa.
Joy in our baile
En Nuestros Abrazos, saludos y cultura.
Joy for who we are and who we are becoming.

We've come a long way, but we have much further to go.

We have come very far, but the road ahead is still long. Each step forward is a victory, but we must remember that the journey is not yet complete. While the progress we've made is worth celebrating, we cannot allow ourselves to become complacent. As I'm publishing this book a man, brown man is being unfairly arrested. Our voices are being quieted.

It's not enough to have ownership of our own bodies if those bodies are still subject to control, surveillance, and policing by others. It's not enough to be given the right to speak if our voices are silenced through censorship, intimidation, or fear. The forces that seek to hold us back are relentless, and so must our determination to keep moving forward (Alese).

What we know:

We know that this country was built on 500-plus years of racism and racialized oppression (Witynski), and the color white was built as a social construct for dominance over people of color, especially Black people. But each of us has the power to change this.

What I know, My healing voice:

My voice, though singular, echoes with the chorus of generations past.

I know that my voice has scientific relevance.

My oppression has given me valuable resistance skills that can be used for more than just keeping the lights on. I carry hundreds of stories, both known and unknown, in my body.

Even now, typing this, my throat hurts, tears come out, and my fingers begin a dance that I don't even know what they are going to type next, but I know that it's needed.

My voice is many. I knew it as a child when I heard them speaking in tongues in church--I knew what they were saying, I've seen ghosts, I've been dead, I've been raped, I've seen life, I've seen blood, I've passed life, I've been hit, and I've been in love several times.

Healing Activity

Now it's your turn to free your voice. There are so many ways that your story could end. But the real truth is that you have the power to heal, and people need to hear what you have to say about life.

Healing from the Latina perspective often embraces ancestral traditions, spirituality, and communal practices that offer holistic approaches to address deep-rooted trauma. Here are some practical steps inspired by these traditions:

1. Limpias (Spiritual Cleansings)
   - ▶ Purpose: Limpias help remove negative energy, emotional blockages, and spiritual heaviness. It's a ritual of renewal.

▶ How to Perform: Use herbs like sage, rosemary, or rue (ruda). Sweep these over your body from head to toe while setting intentions to release what no longer serves you. A trusted curandera (healer) may perform a limpia in a community setting.

▶ Analyze and take notice of the patterns of your life as part of understanding what energy needs to be cleared.

2. Baños (Herbal Baths)

▶ Purpose: Baños purify the body, mind, and spirit by immersing in waters infused with healing herbs, flowers, and essential oils.

▶ How to Prepare: Fill a tub with warm water and add herbs like lavender for relaxation, basil for protection, rose petals for love, and chamomile for peace. You can also use essential oils like eucalyptus or peppermint.

▶ As you bathe, focus on washing away pain, negative experiences, and self-doubt. Visualize where do you see yourself in three months? What are the new dreams that you could do now? What brings you peace? Post-Bath Ritual: Allow the body to air dry without toweling off, letting the herbs and oils fully absorb.

3. Blessings & Affirmations

▶ Purpose: Words carry power. Blessings and affirmations shift energy and perspective, allowing us to reclaim our worth.

▶ How to Practice: Start your day with an affirmation or a blessing. This can be as simple as "Soy digna de amor y respeto" (I am worthy of love and respect) or "Mi historia es mi poder" (My story is my power). Speak these blessings aloud or write them in a journal.

▶ Community Blessings: Engage in group blessings where family or friends speak positive affirmations over each other. The collective energy reinforces healing.

4. Creating Altars (Ofrendas)

- ▶ Purpose: Altars are sacred spaces where we honor our ancestors, struggles, and resilience. They ground us in our lineage and connect us to something greater.

- ▶ How to Create: Place meaningful objects like candles, photos of loved ones, flowers, and symbols of your cultural roots. Add any items that represent your journey and healing process. It doesn't have to be fancy or costly or even have an aesthetic this is your little space or corner.

- ▶ Use of the Altar: Let it be a space where you offer gratitude, set intentions for healing, and call upon your ancestors for strength. Move things around on your altar to help you make a move on your intention.

5. Journaling as a Curandera Practice

- ▶ Purpose: Writing provides a space for deep introspection and releasing internalized feelings. It's a tool to reclaim your story.

- ▶ How to Practice: Set aside time to write freely about your emotions, experiences, and dreams for the future. Incorporate fun elements like stickers or colors that invite creativity and make the process feel less intimidating.

- ▶ Prompts: Reflect on questions like: What pain am I ready to release? What lessons have I learned from my wounds? How can I transform my pain into power? I know this... 3-5 minutes of timed short writing sprints can do you well. Also, use voice memos or voice to text. Or make a small poster!

6. Healing Through Community (Circles)

- ▶ Purpose: Healing doesn't happen in isolation. Surround yourself with a supportive community that understands your experiences and offers mutual compassion.

▶ How to Practice: Organize healing circles with trusted friends or family. These can be spaces where you share stories, grieve, celebrate, and set collective intentions for healing.

▶ Guided Sessions: Participate in group meditations, collective breathwork, or mindfulness exercises that center on healing.

7. Danza & Movement as Physical Liberation

▶ Purpose: Movement, whether through dance, mindfully taking a walk, or other forms of expression, releases tension and connects you to your body. It's a way to celebrate life and joy.

▶ How to Practice: Engage in traditional dances like folklórico, or find any movement that resonates with you. Mindful walking is walking but intentionally feeling how your heel and foot touch the floor.

▶ Affirmation: As you move, remind yourself, "I am sexy and I'm healing with every step."
Meditation & Breathwork

▶ Purpose: Meditation helps us reconnect with our inner selves, finding peace amidst the noise. Breathwork grounds us, releasing anxiety and tension.

▶ How to Practice: Practice deep breathing exercises daily. Inhale through your nose for four counts, hold for four, and exhale for four. As you breathe, visualize healing energy entering your body and past pain leaving.

▶ Mindfulness: Use this space to center yourself in gratitude and visualize the joy you seek to create.

8. Storytelling & Speaking Your Truth

▶ Purpose: Sharing your story is a radical act of reclaiming your voice and history. It helps transform wounds into wisdom.

- ▶ How to Practice: Find a trusted space where you can share your story through writing, speaking in community circles or theatrical performances. Or make your own video and you don't need or have to share it. Listen to yourself. What can you learn from **what** you say--don't focus and **how** you say it! Let your experiences be a source of strength for yourself for when you are going through a rough patch.

9. Rest & Rejuvenation

- ▶ Purpose: Rest is a radical act, especially in systems devaluing our labor and existence. Rest is essential for healing.

- ▶ How to Practice: Prioritize moments of stillness and restoration. Whether it's taking a day off, napping, or practicing stillness, remind yourself that your worth is not tied to productivity.

These steps are pathways toward healing, reclaiming our stories, and moving toward collective joy. Each step reflects the wisdom of our ancestors while empowering us to transform pain into power and build a future where we thrive. Healing in this way is personal and political—it's an act of resistance.

Bonus Journaling Exercises:

Reflect on your own stories and where they may be coming from. Settle the money mind by checking in with yourself and your body.

The **long-term goal is to let go of negative stories that want to sabotage your progress and impact on the world.** It takes practice to let go of these stories. You can counter the skeleton hand by visualizing a shield or saying, **"No, that's not me; it's not true; I can do this!"**

The **short-term goal is to start developing the tools,** I have outlined throughout this book to help you get back to the present. Begin mapping out your future by creating short-term goals that are easy to measure. Poco a poco. These actions are meant to help you feel safe speaking and using your voice. A great way to start is to write affirmations to help us write a truly empowered narrative.

Here are some examples to inspire you.

Soy Mujer, y soy yo!
Tengo voz, y tengo valor.
I'm safe using my voice.
If I stumble or make mistakes, I am still worthy.
Other people don't define my worth. I define my worth.
I'm worthy of love and acceptance for just existing.
My voice is powerful.
I am beautiful and powerful.

Now, it's your turn:

Finish this sentence: I help people _____, and I enjoy doing this work because _____.

I remember when I was happy doing _____.

Write about how this moment was special for you.

Discussion Questions for Groups

1. How is your organization helping others have innovative experiences that allow them to tell their stories?

2. How are you honoring the communities that your storytellers come from?

3. Are you paying storytellers equitable wages? If not, why?

4. How can you promote or sponsor a storyteller?

+++

I think it's fitting to end this book with a poem I wrote about queenhood. Remember, you have the power, and you have choices even when it seems like there aren't any.

In Silence

I gain in silence
I win in silence
I grow in silence
So when You catch up with my Queenhood, don't be surprised,
I was destined to succeed.
Testing the mic and owning the stage are two different things.
I come from
women who
crossed borders,
scrubbed floors,
and harvested a bounty
so I could have the trophy.

Survived boys who only knew how to shut out light and serve themselves.
Faced their blows and their foolishness with a laugh.

From a statistic to a cipher
From poverty to self-love
From being your chisme
to being my own business

Aquí estoy
a mi no me quitan de aquí

**A mi no me quitan de mi vida
ni de mi felicidad**

Not for me?
Don't worry, we got more than enough.

Enchanted mirrors
Poisoned apples
Prince Charming
I was too awkward to be rescued
I was too abused to be worthy
I was too abandoned to be seen

One day,
One day
she whispered, "believe..."

And I followed her through the woods to school

Skinned my knees
Clawed through the leaves
And I wiped it clean,

My heart.

The End

Ahora Tú: Reflect & Release

NOTES FROM GROUND

Tuesday, January 28, 2025

I wanted to end with an update; that is what I like about self-publishing because it has a nowness that if I were going the traditional route, I would not be able to adjust my ending. Given the new Executive orders to roll back DEI workplace initiatives, I wanted to give an update on how to proceed. These suggestions and advice will apply and serve as lightpost to anyone from an oppressed background when applying for a job. We have all read or heard about the backlash to DEI and the rollback of inclusionary recruitment programs. The workforce landscape is changing rapidly, and I wanted to give you a snapshot of my daily life as a consultant, who works for inclusion and workplace realness and respect. DEI was never going to save us. But the backlash is uncovering the bias and has emboldened people in the workforce to be disrespectful and isolate those who are facing the brunt of abuse. It also has questioned the liberty to manage your company to align with your values. This nudges me to ask--were the workers ever in control?

Long-Term Implications of the Executive Order

The implications of this recent Executive Order on programs like TRIO and social services are severe. The people most affected are those who are Black, Latino, and low-income White individuals who rely on services such as tutoring, support services, and emergency grants to cover particular situations which students of color don't have the financial support system like other students.

Mass Deportations and their affect in reporting workplace trauma

The trauma associated with mass deportations is impacting working Latinas, many of whom are the first in their families to break the cycle of generational poverty. We are silently suffering or in shock. Regardless we push down our emotions and when asked if we are doing okay, we smile back and say, yes. In some cases, we center our white liberal colleagues' feelings and fears to assure them that it will be okay.

I'm not saying we want to be left alone, but if you only have tears for a minute and not the dollars or the votes when we need them, then I would say hold your tears and sympathetic hugs. We need a worthy opponent to this display of oppressive power. We need strategy and safety response systems, food distribution, environmental-based solutions, and disability justice.

Challenges in Reporting Discrimination

We discussed why it is often difficult for Latinas in the workforce to report discrimination. I shared my own experience and how it took multiple incidents before I finally filed a discrimination claim. The fear of losing everything—and the people who rely on them for support—leads many to endure mistreatment. For instance, I dressed up for work. I kept smiling to my community peers so I could keep the job and continue to support my uncle, who was critically ill. I felt that I had to endure the emotional abuse of a nonprofit job that claims social justice, inorder to provide for my extended families' needs.

In an inflationary economy, job security is more crucial than ever, which can cause Latinas to overlook aggression, bullying, and micro-management just to maintain their employment. Don't give up! Or give in! Get prepared now.

Get Support and Regulate Expectations of your Professional Life

Professionals from historically oppressed or underprivileged backgrounds often carry a heavier burden than their peers from wealthier families, as they have more dependents relying on them. They frequently face requests for financial help from family members, whether it's loans, cosigning leases, or being the financial safety net.

Let me be clear: Coming from a wealthy background is not a bad thing. What people want is the opportunity to thrive, hold a job, and work peacefully, regardless of their nationality, immigration status, relationship choices, or gender.

Continuing the Conversation

Just like during the pandemic, I am reaching out to my mentors, supporters, advocates, and sponsors—those who will speak up for me when I'm absent. It's essential to pull together during this time and strengthen our bonds with our support networks.

Today, I had the great pleasure of speaking with Dr. Cheryl Gittens. We discussed my recent LinkedIn post, where I asked for advice on how to provide new words of guidance in light of the recent backlash and pullback from DEI. Earlier this week, Federal agencies were instructed to eliminate race- and gender-focused programs, redefine sex as strictly binary under federal law, and proceed with placing all diversity staff on paid leave ahead of planned layoffs. Federal employees are being urged to report any attempts to disguise diversity, equity, and inclusion (DEI) programs, signaling a strict enforcement approach ahead. This is disheartening; the intention seems to want to control people of color, and push back on initiatives that helped reduce bias.

Background and Significance of Today's Discussion

Dr. Cheryl Gittens has dedicated her career to working with TRIO programs. Dr. Gittens has devoted her career over 30 years, to working with higher education institutions to foster inclusion, opportunity, and access through student programs and services, such as the TRIO programs.

Recently, a Presidential Executive Order was issued that proposes to end federally funded programs in higher education, which could include programs like TRIO. Additionally, this order calls for the cessation of federal funding for social services and assistance for victims. This funding freeze could potentially lead to hundreds of job losses, impacting individuals who may now be questioning their job security.

SAGE WORDS

These notes are from my conversation with Dr. Cheryl Gittens on Tuesday, January 28, 2025, over Zoom.

We talked about the news and how people can support each other in the workplace and what we can do for ourselves during these turbulent times.

She says to me:
"Our country is Evolving ...think of this as a revolving cycle,
"We are thriving,"
"Hold on to your light,"
"Know yourself,"
"Don't get consumed by the job or the title,"
"That's not your ceiling,"
"What you have inside of you is what will help you,"
"You will use the same tools as our ancestors did,"
"Focus on self, Not self perseveration,"
"You are not the job title,"

SAGE WORDS FROM Dr. Cheryl Gittens
We can survive oppressors,"
"We can pick up our tools,"
"In the field,"
"In the house, in the workplace,"
"Tools to build, not to fight back,"
"Or start a war but to build because that is what our people do."
"We were focused on fighting and not building."
"We were focused on the language that would welcome us, like DEI, but that's not going to happen."
"If you've been distracted and focused on the fight,"
"Get re-focused, and use your tools. We need to shine and share our tools."

Dr. Cheryl Gittens' final words of good fortune

▶ "Go underground and educate your people."

▶ "Start mentoring people."

▶ "Tell your stories so your children know their history.

Later on, I attended a talk with LinkedIn ERG Workplace Influencer Hady Mendez, who highlighted several actions that people can do to support each other in the workplace.

I love how she outlines how groups within the organizations can implement meaningful changes to improve workplace culture and be real with employees who are feeling down because of the hostile political environment.

She talked about changing the language but not of position in promoting and sustaining safe workplaces because we know that safe workplaces create efficient and effective teams. From her deck:

- ▶ "If you are a leader in your workplace, set clear group norms, make it okay to be vulnerable, and continue to provide opportunities to create times for advocacy."

- ▶ "How are you ensuring that all voices are being heard in meetings?"

- ▶ "Are you setting ground rules that set good boundaries for personal safety?"

- ▶ "Are you creating a safe environment that encourages people to reach out when they need support?"

I ended the day talking with fellow Disability Justice activist Jesenia from Neurospicey Networking; she told me the following about today's current state of affairs.

- ▶ "They want you to give up before you even try. They want you to quit before you begin to change things."

- ▶ "Don't stop yourself from applying for a job just because DEI is dead, you don't know the future, you might get the job."

She shared with me, to share with you, this quote: "If you stay silent, they will kill you and say you liked it." --**Zora Neale Neale Hurston.**

<u>Cited Resources for the New Proposed Policies</u>

<u>https://www.cnn.com/2025/01/27/politics/white-house-pauses-federal-grants-loan-disbursement/index.html</u>

And <u>https://www.whitehouse.gov/presidential-actions/2025/01/initial-rescissions-of-harmful-executive-orders-and-actions/</u>

Thank you to my three guests and virtual mentors:

Hady Mendez, Latina ERG Consultant <u>https://www.linkedin.com/in/hadymendez/</u>

Dr. Cheryl B. Gittens, Consultant, <u>https://www.linkedin.com/in/dr-cheryl-b-gittens-b6a40a220/</u>

Disabilities Advocate, Speaker, and Consultant, Jesenia M.

<u>https://www.linkedin.com/in/jeseniam/</u>

CLOSING REMARKS

Become a worthy opponent.

There is a mass firing going on right now.

We all deserve to be respected and comfortable in our workplace. That is a human right.

People are being forced to hide or live in fear while driving. There's a Latina Anne Frank hiding from ICE in the attic. Latino kids are learning to remain calm, show their hands, maintain silence, and call a lawyer. How do we move from here? Forward? Under? Above? Where is it safe? I purpose through.

We must see through this fire and patterns of chaos, and become that worthy opponent to fear and hate. Does it mean getting healthy? It could. I know that not everyone is or wants to be an activist. THAT'S okay! As a white girlfriend told me over the weekend at a local dive bar, it's about morality. What is in your corazón? Where is your corazón? Tend to your heart.

Uncovering who you are through writing or other cleansing of the soul practices will help you. This time, we have to do this with love. Radical self-love. How do we cultivate that type of love?

Project your joy. Protect your talents and work. You can do that by networking for a new job. I heard about this new group called "Never Search Alone" (https://www.phyl.org/). Public libraries are still places to find and refine your skills. Don't give up, your talents, skills, and knowledge are needed in your town, city, or country!

Writing this book has been a healing ritual. Allowing myself to dive into the different ways I was harassed, how I found friendships, took a university-level continuing education course, and participated in the racial uprising after the murder of George Floyd. I know I've talked about it already in this book, but I think it's crucial now that we're at the end, to talk about why I wrote this book.

I wrote this book for women, for Latinas, for Black women, for Brown women, for Queer/Trans women, for First Gen folks, and Immigrant women who have faced discrimination in the workplace. I wrote this for mujeres who followed their hearts to work for a nonprofit organization that was white-led, and that ultimately did not have their best interests in mind. I wrote this book for women of color who have been tokenized and abused in the business sector. More importantly, though, I wrote this so that we become **a worthy opponent of racism and the structures that sustain workplace discrimination, the systems that want to silence our voices.**

What I'm asking you to do is to free your voice and become a worthy opponent of racism. Your voice is not just important; it's crucial. Your experiences, your struggles, and your resilience are what make this country better. Rescue yourself so that you can guide others and be an example.

Why is this book important? Because this book came with sacrifice. Most importantly, this book is essential because I hope you will find the courage to file a complaint. Even if you don't go through it, even if you don't win the case, you did it—you raised the bar. This book is essential because it's a testimony that no matter how many times you get pushed down or shoved to the side, you can get up with your head held high, walk into any room, and know your presence has a history that no one can take away.

This book is intentionally short and meant to be read in transit. It's meant to be opened at different times. It's meant to be part of a workshop. This book is intended to be part of a group discussion to be given away at conferences to educate government officials who work in civil rights departments to help encourage and inspire Equal Opportunity City commissioners around the nation. It's meant to inspire you. Notice that I have hardly used the word victim throughout the whole book.

Of course, we are victims, and that goes without saying. We were lucky enough to live past the age of 18 without being shot or killed, dying of overdose, or suicide. I was not going to give us a book in which the word victim would be centered. I wanted to provide you with the gift of being a Guerrera, a warrior, a woman, a worthy opponent with the strategies to heal and come back stronger with love.

This book has transformed me personally. I've held on to this story for too long. I'm so glad I can let it go. If it brings you joy, gives you a reflection, and inspires you, my work is done. I've introduced you to people in my family. I've introduced you to the Devils of my life, and my hope is that you will continue the tradition of the circle and create your own circle. Remember, your story is powerful, and sharing it can empower others, inspiring them to speak out and fight against discrimination.

What new dreams do you have for the future?

ABOUT THE AUTHOR:

Photo credit: Mayra Linares

"To me, being a poeta means to be able to catch fires, to bring forth something from labor and sweat, to have enough when there's not a lot."

Araceli Esparza draws from the historical work of Gloria Anzaldua, bell hooks, Aurora Levins Morales, critical race theory through a Chicana lens, intersectionality, social entrepreneurship, and social justice. She founded Midwest Mujeres Collective to help Latinas and women expand their networks and grow their businesses or professional knowledge.

As a guiding force for companies, nonprofits, and individuals, she helps them create authentic outreach and engagement workshops and consulting strategies that positively impact marginalized communities. Named 2024 Wisconsin's Most Influential Latina, Araceli empowers Latinas to tell their stories. As a motivational speaker and consultant for libraries, historical sites, and nonprofit organizations, she guides these entities to build authentic relationships with communities, fostering sustainable leadership cycles.

Araceli Esparza's personal interests provide a glimpse into her life beyond her professional endeavors. Born and raised in Madison, WI, to migrant farmworker parents from Guanajuato, Mexico, she draws strength from her roots. Araceli is a graduate of the University of Minnesota and Hamline University with a Master of Fine Arts in Creative Writing for Children. In her free time, she enjoys writing picture books and poetry, a passion that reflects her creative spirit and commitment to storytelling.

For Bookings, email: info@araceliesparza.com

Discover about my work: **www.araceliesparza.com/about**

Instagram: @araceliesparza_speaker

LinkedIn: https://www.linkedin.com/in/araceliesparza/

Araceli's Spotify playlist From the WOC Collective.

Araceli's Linktree

<u>Resources</u>

When in crisis or Mental Helath needs:

Call or text 988 to connect with a trained crisis counselor 24/7.

Call 1-800-662-HELP (4357) or text your 5-digit ZIP Code to 435748 (HELP4U) for treatment referral and information 24/7

 **The Pastor who listened to me:** https://lilada.org/

 **The Trans Influencer/Comedian who listened and coached me:**
https://dinanina.com/

 **Project LETS is a national grassroots organization and movement led by and for folks with lived experience of mental illness/madness, Disability, trauma, & neurodivergence.**
https://projectlets.org/resources

 **Unpacking Trauma and trauma-theory through an Indigenous lens**
https://www.jessicabarudin.com/blog/trauma-indigenous-lens

 **Decolonizing Trauma Work: Indigenous Stories and Strategies**
https://a.co/d/2tQqSOt

 **The Pain We Carry: Healing from Complex PTSD for People of Color**
https://a.co/d/itcplWd

 **End Workplace Abuse**
https://endworkplaceabuse.com/

 **U.S. Equal Employment Opportunities Commission**
https://www.eeoc.gov

 **Discrimination and Racism Resources**
https://myusf.usfca.edu/caps/self-help-resources/discrimination

American Civil Liberties Union
https://www.aclu.org/

BEST PRACTICES AND TIPS FOR EMPLOYEES
https://www.eeoc.gov/initiatives/e-race/best-practices-and-tips-employees

UNIDOS US, they are a national organization challenging the social, economic, and political barriers that affect Latinos in the United States across a range of key issues
https://unidosus.org/issues/civil-rights-and-racial-equity/

I truly believe in the power of Music, here is beautiful Spotify playlist from mi amiga Purple! Her Women of Color Group:
https://woc-sister-collective.squarespace.com/

Playlist for healing:
https://open.spotify.com/playlist/1H54DKR1f1B-2VpDdgWLOdE?si=da2daf245c584f56

Midwest Mujeres! Join our group of networking and storytelling courses!
www.midwestmujeres.com

My Linktree!
https://linktr.ee/araceliesparza_speaker

Listen to my work on Wisconsin Life:
https://wisconsinlife.org/story/grandmother-recalled-in-the-earthy-smell-of-beets/

My animated short!
https://youtu.be/hO_qPQv7d6w?si=Z2hygsukp2sx_t5i

LULAC: League of United Latin American Citizens
https://lulac.org/

 **MALDEF (Mexican American Legal Defense and Educational Fund) is the leading civil rights voice of the Latino community.**
https://www.maldef.org/about/mission/

 **NALEO is a non-partisan organization that facilitates full Latino participation in the American political process, from citizenship to public service.**
https://naleo.org/

 **The Leadership Conference on Civil and Human Rights**
https://civilrights.org/value/fighting-hate-bias/

Best Resource
Trusted Friends and Family
And
You!

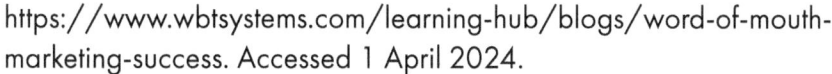

WORKS CITED

December 2019. https://hbr.org/2019/11/how-the-best-bosses-interrupt-bias-on-their-teams.

Wikipedia, 2021.

https://www.wbtsystems.com/learning-hub/blogs/word-of-mouth-marketing-success. Accessed 1 April 2024.

How to Emulate the Word-of-Mouth Marketing Success of USF's Popular DEI Certificate Program, https://www.wbtsystems.com/learning-hub/blogs/word-of-mouth-marketing-success. Accessed 1 April 2024.

Anzaldua, Gloria E. "Speaking In Tongues: A Letter To 3rd World Women Writers." March 2024.

https://hamtramckfreeschool.files.wordpress.com/2014/05/anzalducc81a-gloria-this-bridge-called-my-back-dragged.pdf.

Cleveland Clinic. (2023). *Body Scan Meditation for Beginners: How To Make the Mind/Body Connection.*

DiDio, Laura. "Gender Bias, Equal Pay and Harassment Still Pervasive for Women STEM Professionals." *TechChannel*, 2 June 2022, https://techchannel.com/Trends/06/2022/gender-bias-stem. Accessed 1 April 2024.

Gee, Alex, and Michelle Stocker. "Justified anger: Rev. Alex Gee says Madison is failing its African-American community." *The Cap Times*, 18 December 2013, https://captimes.com/news/local/city-life/justified-anger-rev-alex-gee-says-madison-is-failing-its-african-american-community/article_2556653d-4ac1-5a54-aee5-9619c94d36ff.html. Accessed 1 April 2024.

"The gender pay gap is even worse for Latinas with college degrees." CNBC, 5 October 2023, https://www.cnbc.com/2023/10/05/the-gender-pay-gap-is-even-worse-for-latinas-with-college-degrees.html. Accessed 1 April 2024.

"George Floyd Square occupied protest." Wikipedia, https://en.wikipedia.org/wiki/George_Floyd_Square_occupied_protest. Accessed 1 April 2024.

"Half of U.S Latinos experienced some form of discrimination during the first year of the pandemic." Pew Research Center, 4 November 2021, https://www.pewresearch.org/hispanic/2021/11/04/half-of-u-s-latinos-experienced-some-form-of-discrimination-during-the-first-year-of-the-pandemic/. Accessed 1 April 2024.

Hauge, Ruthie, and Nicholas Garton. "Madison officer who killed Tony Robinson won't be charged, judge rules." The Cap Times, 30 June 2023, https://captimes.com/news/community/madison-officer-who-killed-tony-robinson-wont-be-charged-judge-rules/article_8032d70d-f879-564a-9728-722cf94b6f81.html. Accessed 1 April 2024.

Levin Morales, Aurora. "The Historian as Curandera." Institute for Cultural Activism, https://jsri.msu.edu/upload/working-papers/wp40.pdf.

M, Jesenia. "Building Businesses with an Anti-Capitalist Focus." Calling Up Justice!, 2 August 2023, https://callingupjustice.com/building-businesses-with-an-anti-capitalist-focus/. Accessed 1 April 2024.

Ramos, George. "Thousands of Latinos March in Washington." 13 Oct 1996, https://www.latimes.com/archives/la-xpm-1996-10-13-mn-53507-story.html. Accessed 2 4 2024.

Romo Edelman, Claudia. Hispanic Stars Rising: The New Face of Power. Fig Factor Media Publishing, 2020.

"Steve Jobs on Creativity." *Farnam Street Blog*, https://fs.blog/
steve-jobs-on-creativity/#:~:text=Creativity%20is%20just%20
connecting%20things,had%20and%20synthesize%20new%20
things.

University of Arizona. (n.d.). *Grounding & Breathing Exercises for
Calming Your Nervous System*. https://caps.arizona.edu/grounding

U.S. Equal Employment Opportunity Commission. *Race and Color
Discrimination*, U.S. Equal Employment Opportunity Commission, https://
www.eeoc.gov/racecolor-discrimination.

Williams, Joan C. "How the Best Bosses Interrupt Bias on Their Teams."
Harvard Business Review, 2019, https://hbr.org/2019/11/how-the-best-
bosses-interrupt-bias-on-their-teams. Accessed 1 April 2024.

Witynski, Max. "For Ta-Nehisi Coates, telling the truth about America
means confronting Black oppression." *UChicago News*, 3 June 2021,
https://news.uchicago.edu/story/ta-nehisi-coates-telling-truth-about-
america-means-confronting-black-oppression. Accessed 1 April 2024.

Whitney Alese, Instagram post. Paraphrased with permission.

Yellow Medicine Journal. A Journal of Indigenous Literature, Art, and
Thought. "Walk in Silence." *Yellow Medicine Journal*, vol. 2, no. 20, 2022,
p. 60.

www.ingramcontent.com/pod-product-compliance
Lightning Source LLC
Chambersburg PA
CBHW071519120626
46550CB00006B/2278